HIGH FLYERS

15
INSPIRING WOMEN AVIATORS and ASTRONAUTS

ANN McCALLUM STAATS

T0284326

CHICAGO
REVIEW
PRESS

To my family, once again.
I love you to outer space and back.

Contents

Introduction   vii

Part I   Elevated (10,000—18,000 Feet)   1

1   Brooke Roman: Flying over Alaska   2
2   Tammy Duckworth: Pilot Turned Politician   15
3   Edgora McEwan: On the Rise   28
4   Dede Murawsky: Horseback to Medevac   40
5   Anne Macdonald: A Rank Above   52

Part II   Altitude (30,000—45,000 Feet)   65

6   Tammie Jo Shults: Flying Past the Noes   66
7   Katie Higgins Cook: Blue Angel Icon   79
8   Olga Custodio: Where There's a Will   93
9   Kimberly Scott Ford: The Glide-Path Forward   105
10   Ronaqua Russell: *Semper Paratus*—Always Ready   118

Part III   Outside Earth (62+ Miles)   131

11   Mae Jemison: No Limits   132
12   Ellen Ochoa: Music Among the Stars   145

13   Samantha Cristoforetti: Home in Space   158

14   Karen Nyberg: Space Artist   172

15   Anousheh Ansari: Entrepreneur in Space   185

Afterword   199

Acknowledgments   202

Notes   204

Introduction

They did *what*?

They went *where*?

The women in this book are no timid back-seaters. They are high-flying go-getters who have chosen careers in unconventional—but incredibly rewarding—airspace or beyond. These are real women from humble backgrounds who dared to dream big. They are a hot-air balloonist, a helicopter pilot turned senator, military officers, astronauts, commercial aviators, and more. They are brave, bold dreamers and doers who fly outside the lines.

From the moment I first approached the subjects in this book, I knew I'd tapped into something extraordinary. That feeling grew as I interviewed each subject and delved into further research. Here were seemingly everyday women, people whose childhoods gave little clue to the astounding accomplishments that would come later in life. Of course, there *are* always hints, however small. As a child, when Anousheh Ansari gazed at the stars from her grandparents' balcony, it was a catalyst to a lifelong devotion to space exploration. When young Kimberly Scott Ford attended a Blue Angels jet demonstration exhibit, she fell in love with the idea of becoming a pilot. As Tammie Jo Shults watched the jet training exercises over Holloman Air Force Base near her family's home in New Mexico, she yearned to try flying herself.

For each of these women the path to success was never smooth, nor easy. All of them have faltered, sometimes because of money, other times because of societal norms or lack of encouragement and support. In every case, however, these women *did* achieve what they set out to do. There were risks—and still are—but it was worth it. From the airspace on Earth to a vastness of no air off-planet, *High Flyers* profiles a collection of remarkable women who believed, despite the odds, that soaring is possible.

Here is a bird's-eye view of their stories.

Part I
Elevated
(10,000—18,000 Feet)

1

Brooke Roman: Flying over Alaska

Brooke Roman was being chased by a bear. Moments before, she had been taking a friend's two dogs for a walk along a pristine trail near Talkeetna, Alaska, a historic town at the base of America's tallest mountain, Mount Denali.

Brooke was relishing the lack of human-made noise and the raw beauty of the outdoors. Initially, she thought that the disturbance in the woods beside her was a moose. Boomer, a fearless golden retriever, broke away and raced after whatever it was before Brooke could stop him.

"Come back!"

Seconds later, Boomer did come back, tail between his legs as he blew past Brooke. He streaked down the trail taking the second dog with him. Brooke was alone on the trail when a very annoyed grizzly bear crashed from the woods. It was a mama bear, and she was not happy to have had her young cubs threatened.

Adrenaline thrumming through her, Brooke tried to remember everything she knew about surviving a grizzly bear attack. *Do not run. Do not look the bear directly in the eyes. Back away slowly. If attacked, play dead in the fetal position and protect your organs. Stay calm.*

This last advice was especially difficult, but Brooke stood her ground. Then she stepped away, gently and slowly. Thankfully, after a standoff that lasted several seconds, the bear lost interest and lumbered away. Alone on the trail once more, Brooke made her way back to her car on shaking legs. There, after finding and securing the dogs, she sat behind the wheel and reflected on her decision to move to Alaska to become a bush pilot. *Was it worth the many risks?*

Life in the United States' northernmost state included many dangers. Aside from potential wildlife encounters, there was the harsh weather, extreme cold, and isolation. Brooke started up the car. *But the rewards are greater than the risks*, she told herself. Living—and flying—in Alaska was exactly what she wanted to do with her life. Despite the grizzly bear encounter and the other very real hazards, she knew she had made the right choice.

The Great Land

The name Alaska comes from the Aleut word *Alyeska*. Today, approximately 740,000 people including about 224 different indigenous tribes call Alaska home. America's largest state is 665,384 square miles of tundra, forests, rivers, lakes, volcanoes, and towering mountains. Denali is the continent's highest peak at 20,320 feet above sea level.

With 34,000 miles of coastline, 3,000 rivers, and 3 million lakes, Alaska dwarfs her southern states. Though the climate varies considerably in this huge state, in some places, extreme temperatures can provide a real challenge to survival. The coldest temperature on record is a bone-chilling 80 degrees Fahrenheit below zero (-62.2° Celsius), recorded in 1971 at Prospect Creek. Alaska is a true wilderness with an average of only 1.3 people per square mile. With much of the state inaccessible by car, the population depends on aircraft for transportation of people and supplies.

Brooke Roman wasn't born in Alaska. Nor does she have any family there. Instead, she grew up in Nixa, Missouri, a self-proclaimed nerdy kid with a keen sense of adventure. She loved to challenge herself, like when she raced around the house with a stopwatch to try and improve her time. She enjoyed sports, especially wakeboarding, swimming, tubing, and boating with her family. She never dreamed of being a pilot.

When Brooke was younger, she wanted to be a doctor. In high school she joined a program called Medical Explorers. As part of the team of students, she had the opportunity to watch surgeries at a local hospital. Once she even observed an autopsy and was fascinated by what she learned. She looked forward to a medical career, and it seemed like her life's path was set. Or was it?

Brooke's family took a vacation once a year by airplane. Each time she flew, curiosity tugged at Brooke. What was it like in the cockpit of the plane? What would it be like to travel in front and be the one in charge of flying? The idea took root, tugging at her and opening up a new potential career track. One day Brooke made a life-altering decision. She looked into what it would take to become a pilot.

Brooke went to college. When she graduated from Kansas State University, she earned a bachelor's degree not in pre-med, but in aeronautical technology. Launched on this new path, Brooke completed an internship with Southwest Airlines and was now on track to becoming a commercial pilot. Once again, fate intervened.

The AirVenture Airshow located in Oshkosh, Wisconsin, is an annual event dubbed "The World's Greatest Aviation Celebration." Brooke and her friends made plans to attend. They would camp under the wing of one friend's small private plane and immerse themselves in several days of aviation performances and displays. Brooke couldn't wait!

Once at the airshow, Brooke noticed a number of booths that had been set up for various products and companies. One in particular caught her interest. It was the Seaplane Pilots Association, and the organization was giving away a free scholarship to earn a seaplane rating, a license to fly a plane that could take off and land on water. Intrigued, Brooke scrounged up a piece of paper and filled out an application. Later, she was surprised and ecstatic to learn that she'd won the scholarship. Now she had her choice of where to go to take the training. She chose Alaska.

Already armed with her commercial pilot's license, earning the seaplane qualification was a relatively quick add-on. Brooke would train in Talkeetna at Alaska Floats and Skis. The facility included a course for learning to land bush planes. Instead of touching down on a runway, these planes were equipped for wilderness landings on either water or snow. Depending on their destination, they were outfitted with pontoons or skis instead of regular landing gear. They might also be equipped with "bush wheels," large, 35-inch tires that made landing on tundra or gravel bars possible.

To earn the seaplane rating, Brooke would spend class time learning the unique techniques needed to land on water in addition to several hours of practical experience in the air. She would also need to pass a "check" flight where she would be evaluated and ultimately deemed ready for obtaining the certification. The best part was that Brooke would be learning from legendary Don Lee, a venerable and highly respected local bush pilot, an expert at flying in the Alaskan wilderness. It was going to be great!

Brooke flew into Anchorage, the largest city in Alaska. From there, it was approximately 100 miles north by car to Christiansen Lake, home base for Alaska Floats and Skis. There was a wooden sign with the company's name announcing the resort. Brooke looked past the buildings to the several planes resting on the water, their pontoons keeping them afloat. Her training would start the next day.

Flying in Alaska was far different from the flying Brooke was used to. In her experience, there was always a runway. There were air traffic controllers and, no matter how small the airfield, she had always landed on a tarmac. Alaska's bush pilots had no such luxury—or constraint. Here, with few roads and fewer airstrips, Don showed Brooke the spectacular variety of off-airport landing and takeoff locations that were possible for his fleet of planes. Suddenly, she could visit places so remote that they were otherwise inaccessible to humans. It was a freedom and privilege that was awe-inspiring.

Brooke soon immersed herself in learning—and practicing—the unique techniques required for float plane operations. She started each training flight by checking over the plane. Were the floats damaged? Were there any leaks? Did she need to pump water from the compartmentalized sections of either float? She checked the propeller next. Had it sustained any damage from the unconventional landings? Was it in good shape? Brooke went through a detailed checklist every time she flew. She reminded herself that, when flying, everything was great—until it wasn't. Preflight safety checks were critical.

Once in the pilot's seat, Brooke was constantly monitoring the conditions inside and outside of the plane. How much fuel did she have left? Was it enough to get to her destination? Were the instruments on her dashboard working properly? What was the weather like not only where she was, but also where she was headed? In Alaska, conditions could change rapidly. Brooke couldn't rely exclusively on the weather forecast. Her awareness of current and potential conditions could mean the difference between life and death.

Brooke's seaplane training passed quickly. She learned to taxi on the water, popping the flaps and achieving liftoff. She practiced more advanced techniques like single float takeoffs. This procedure was helpful because there was always a tremendous drag on the plane as it skimmed across a body of water. If Brooke could lift one float up, that resistance was reduced by half. She mastered turn takeoffs, too. These were necessary when there wasn't enough room on a body of water for a straight path ahead. When she went up for her check flight—the run that would qualify her for the seaplane rating—she passed easily. Next, Don offered her a job.

Brooke didn't immediately accept Don's offer, tempted as she was. She still had her dream of becoming a commercial airline pilot, maybe for Southwest Airlines. . . . Flying for a commercial airline company was a more prestigious job. Plus, that option would certainly pay better, too. Despite her other choices, Brooke didn't take long to decide.

After Brooke accepted Don's offer, some people thought she was foolish to turn down the benefits of a commercial airline job. But Brooke had fallen in love with Alaska, and she knew the decision was right for her. For the next three years she worked as a flight instructor. She built up flight hours and mastered the unique techniques of flying into remote areas and landing on various terrain. Then she was offered another opportunity. She could fly drones for the US military.

Much as Brooke loved her job, it had served as a stepping-stone to whatever came next. But did she want to leave Alaska to fly drones? The pay alone was over four times what she was currently making. Brooke did some serious soul-searching. She thought about the disadvantages of living in Alaska but then reflected on the sense of adventure and the opportunities to explore that living here offered. She turned down the drone job and applied to be a pilot for an oil company working from Alaska's North Slope, the northern shore of the state.

When Brooke accepted the job with the oil company, she learned that she would fly a twin otter, a double turboprop engine plane. Her job was to transport people and equipment for the company. She would work a one-week-on, one-week-off schedule. It was perfect.

Not Without an Escort

Life on Alaska's North Slope is like nowhere else on Earth. Without earning the proper certification, people are discouraged from traveling there without an experienced escort. The risks are simply too great for those who are unaccustomed to the conditions. These dangers range from extreme weather to oil field hazards to aggressive wildlife, especially polar bears. While these bears would normally stay mostly on ice floes, the changing climate has decreased the available ice, so these apex predators have increasingly taken up residence on land. Grizzly bears can be aggressive toward humans if they feel threatened, but polar bears will actively seek out humans as a food source. It is necessary for people to be constantly vigilant. In the oil camps there are also occupational hazards. Safety training is imperative when working around heavy equipment and volatile substances. To work in this environment, employees are required to pass a North Slope Training Cooperative (NSTC) class.

Today when she's not working, Brooke's home is in Talkeetna. Several of her coworkers live even farther away; some fly up from Texas or Los Angeles, though theirs is a two-week on/two-week off rotation. When she's on the job, Brooke stays in a room at the oil company's base camp. There are about 600 people on campus, and though there are other women, she is currently the only female pilot. Within the camp, she describes the conditions as wonderful. There are three hot meals provided each day, and entertainment rooms such as a music room, gym, and small movie theater are great for off-hours. Outside is a different story—the environment is among the harshest of anywhere on Earth.

Work continues, no matter the season or the conditions outside. In the winter months there is no sunlight for three months. Temperatures regularly fall to 45 degrees Fahrenheit below zero (–43 degrees Celsius), and with the wind chill, it can feel even colder. Because of this, land vehicles are kept running 24/7. If they were turned off, engines would freeze and break. To protect against the cold, the planes are kept in hangars. Whenever Brooke flies, her plane is equipped with safety gear in case of a crash or getting stuck in the wilderness. Every plane includes sleeping bags, food, water packets, matches, an ax or hatchet, and bug spray—mosquitoes are a real hazard during the summer months.

Brooke's workday starts early. Usually up by 6:30 AM, Brooke is at her preflight briefing by 8:30. This is the time when she studies the day's weather patterns, goes over safety procedures, and makes sure that the plane she'll be flying is prepared. Here, she finds out what she'll be doing that day, too. Often it's transporting people and equipment to various locations in the oil field. With only about 10 percent of the area accessible by road, people rely on air transportation to get from one point to another. They also build ice roads.

Every winter, engineers build roads and runways made from ice. This allows vehicles and aircraft to travel to new places to tap into additional oil reserves. Whenever Brooke lands her plane on one of these ice runways, she uses various techniques to slow and stop on the slick surface. What she doesn't do is slam on the brakes—this would send the plane skidding out of control.

Aside from transporting crew and cargo, sometimes Brooke has a different mission. One of these is to track polar bears. According to the law, companies may not construct roads too close to polar bear dens. In order to preserve these endangered creatures, people must make every effort not to alter the natural course of the bears' lives. But since it's often impossible to see where a polar bear has built a snow cave, Brooke sometimes flies a scientist from the Bureau of Land Management to locate these dens. This science expert may use an infrared camera to locate heat sources beneath the snow. It's one way of finding an otherwise impossible-to-see polar bear's den.

To Brooke, life in Alaska is full of awe and gratitude. She loves the adventure of what she's doing, but she also has a deep respect for the state's remote locations. When she touches down on an isolated patch of wilderness where she's never been before, she often reflects, "There's a solid chance no other person has stepped on this spot." Alaska is a magical, majestic place. Despite the very real hardships of living there, for Brooke, the draw of Alaska's land and people far outweighs the challenges.

She says, "I found the place I want to stay."

Crash Survival

Though no pilot wants to expect it, accidents *do* happen. Therefore, experienced pilots in Alaska will take steps to ensure the survival of themselves and their passengers should their plane crash or break down away from civilization. Perhaps most important is to have a way to signal for help—if the plane does go down, a rescue team needs to know exactly where to locate the survivors as soon as possible. The next priorities are for shelter, medical attention, fire, and food and water. While all planes are required to have basic survival gear on board such as five days' worth of equipment and rations, pilots know to wear a survival vest or keep vital equipment in their pockets. If the plane crashes and it is imperative to get out fast, having stocked pockets can save lives. Pilots train regularly for emergencies, planning for the worst-case scenario.

Follow Brooke Roman Online

Website: https://ladieslovetaildraggers.com/brooke -roman-alaska/

Instagram: @brookieroman

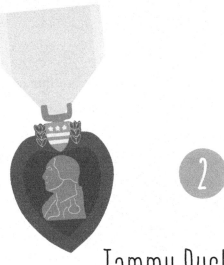

Tammy Duckworth:
Pilot Turned Politician

"Many people who are severely wounded have their initial fears of a life destroyed replaced by the understanding that they can do just about anything."

An Assistant Secretary in the Department of Veteran Affairs, Ladda Tammy Duckworth was at the Washington Convention Center on May 18, 2009, to participate in a ceremony held by the US Postal Service. She was not yet a US Senator—that would come later.

The purpose of the day's event was to commemorate the reissue of the Purple Heart stamp, a tribute to the recipients of this prestigious award. Tammy was speaking from experience and her own heart. She had earned this medal after sustaining unthinkable injuries that nearly killed her. On November 12, 2004, Tammy had been flying a Black Hawk helicopter in Iraq.

It was supposed to be a routine flight—except that nothing in the war in Iraq was ever routine.

The Purple Heart is awarded to those who are wounded or killed in combat service to the United States. It is the oldest military honor still bestowed, and one of the most chilling. As Tammy stood at the podium, she stood tall, but not on her own two legs. Instead, two prosthetic devices helped her stay upright. As she spoke to the crowd in front of her, she recalled when she lost both her legs.

On the day of the attack, Tammy was one of two pilots—four crewmembers altogether—in the helicopter commonly referred to as the Black Hawk. She had been in Iraq for eight months and had already put in over 120 hours of combat flying. They were on their way back to base to end their day when a radio call came in. The mission was simple: First Cavalry Division requested they fly approximately 30 miles to pick up a group of soldiers at Camp Taji, a military base north of Baghdad. As was the rule, they were flying in pairs. A second helicopter flew behind them.

When Tammy's crew arrived at Camp Taji, most of the soldiers were already gone. The only one left, a colonel who had arrived in Iraq that day, climbed into the second helicopter. The two aircraft took off, flying low over the trees, intent on getting back to where they were stationed in Balad. One minute the flight was normal, fun even. Then, suddenly, it wasn't. Someone on the ground was shooting at them.

An unlucky strike hit Tammy's helicopter. Insurgents had fired on them with a rocket propelled grenade, an RPG. Tammy fought to help land the broken helicopter. If they didn't get it on the ground soon, they would crash and likely all die. She scanned the ground. There! An opening appeared between the palm trees. She tried to work the control pedals below with her feet, but nothing was responding. She didn't realize until later the true extent of her injuries below her waist.

Tammy struggled to remain conscious so she could help land the helicopter. Beside her, Dan Milberg, the second pilot in the cockpit, had taken over the controls. The priority was to get them on the ground. Next was to secure the area and treat the injuries of the crew. He glanced at Tammy and assumed she was dead—or soon would be.

The helicopter came to a rest in the tall grass. Tammy, still conscious, knew the situation was bad, though she didn't realize just how dire things were until much later. The last thing she remembers is attempting to reach up to shut off the engines, a safety precaution to prevent the aircraft from being engulfed in flames. She blacked out before she had the chance.

With the crew from the second helicopter helping, Dan carried the two other injured crewmembers to the undamaged aircraft. Specialist Kurt Hanneman had been shot in his tailbone. Sergeant Chris Fierce had a critical leg injury. They needed to get Kurt and Chris to the hospital *ASAP*. Taking precious minutes, Dan came back for Tammy's body. It wasn't until they were in the air that, to everyone's surprise, they realized that Tammy was still alive. But for how long?

At first, survival came down to a moment-by-moment struggle. Ultimately, Tammy ended up losing her full right leg and the portion below her knee on the left side. She nearly lost her arm, too, but, after multiple surgeries, the doctors were able to save that at least. As soon as she was deemed stable enough, Tammy was flown to Walter Reed Medical Base, an army hospital located in Bethesda, Maryland. It would take over a year of determination and excruciating pain before she was healed enough to go home.

Years later, as Tammy stood at the podium at the Postal Service ceremony, a sense of purpose and accomplishment filled what was left of her body. She had achieved a lot since the attack. While it had been exceptionally difficult and many things were still extremely challenging for her, she reflected that, disabled or not, she still had a lot to contribute to the world.

Operation Iraqi Freedom

After the 9/11 attacks where 19 terrorists hijacked four planes and flew them into various US targets, President George W. Bush announced a global "War on Terror." As part of this, US and coalition forces gave Iraq's leader, Saddam Hussein, an ultimatum: step down and leave

Iraq or face military action. On March 19, 2003, airstrikes against Saddam Hussein's palace and other military targets commenced. Thousands of US and coalition soldiers deployed to Iraq to begin "Operation Iraqi Freedom." Hussein fled but was eventually found and put on trial. Convicted of various crimes, he was sentenced to death by an Iraqi court. Finally, in 2010, the last US combat brigade left Iraq, and the mission was renamed "Operation New Dawn" with the new objective of helping Iraqi citizens secure their country and move forward.

Ladda Tammy Duckworth was born on March 12, 1968, in Bangkok, Thailand, to a Thai-Chinese mother and an American father. When she was a child, Tammy's family moved a lot. Her father, Frank, was a retired marine and, at first, the family lived in various parts of Southeast Asia while Frank took on various jobs, including work for the United Nations. Tammy learned to speak Thai and Indonesian along with English. But life wasn't always easy. For a while Tammy's family lived in Cambodia when the country was going through a violent civil war, though luckily, as a child, Tammy wasn't aware of the high degree of danger. Finally, just before things got really bad, Tammy, her brother, Tom, and her mother left. Evacuating via US military transport, Frank soon followed.

For a time, the Duckworths did well, now living in Indonesia. But when Frank lost a string of new jobs, the family eventually plunged into poverty. Finally, desperate and nearly broke, Frank borrowed enough money for three tickets to Hawaii. As soon as she could, Tammy's mother would join her husband and two children. It was many months before she did.

Tammy, now in her senior year, did well at McKinley High School in Honolulu. But as well as she was doing in school, her family's financial situation was getting worse. Tammy and Tom got free breakfast and lunch at school, but the family had to rely on food stamps for other meals. Out of survival, Tammy took on various part-time jobs, including handing out flyers and selling flowers by the side of the road. It was exhausting, but her efforts did pay off—the money helped her family scrape by.

Tammy knew she wanted to go to college, the key to getting out of poverty. Her family scrimped and saved further so she could attend the University of Hawaii. For example, to save on bus fare, her parents started walking places. Tammy also applied for loans and grants, initially thinking she would become a marine biologist. Instead, in 1989 she graduated with a bachelor's degree in political science.

Tammy hadn't yet considered becoming a pilot. Instead, she wondered about becoming a linguist or perhaps a foreign ambassador. After all, she had lived overseas and was proficient at different languages. For now, she knew she wanted to keep studying, so she enrolled at George Washington University in

Washington, DC, to earn a master's degree in international affairs. While there, her life took a new turn. After being laid off from her latest part-time job, a friend suggested Tammy join the Reserve Officer Training Corps (ROTC). The move set her future in motion.

Tammy loved the military. Here, advancement was earned by those who were most capable—money and background didn't matter. Plus, with a deeply engrained sense of honor and service, it was an excellent way for Tammy to contribute. It was also in ROTC where she met her future husband, Bryan Bowlsbey. Like her, he was a cadet, though one year further along.

While Tammy was finishing up her master's degree, another life choice opened up. Having earned a fellowship for Asian American students, she was working in a museum. Her boss, Dr. Paul Taylor, suggested she pursue a doctorate degree at Northern Illinois University (NIU) with a goal of working for the United Nations someday. NIU had an excellent program for Southeast Asian studies, he told her.

Initially Tammy wasn't interested in visiting, let alone attending, such a faraway university. But Dr. Taylor persisted, and she finally agreed to drive to NIU. To her surprise—but not his—Tammy loved Illinois. Later, first as a Representative and then Senator for the state, she reflected on the chance decision she'd made to make Illinois her home.

Graduating from ROTC, Tammy earned her commission in 1992. Initially she thought she would work as a linguist but soon realized that it was only fair that she assume the same risk as some of the men in her unit. The problem was that, at the time, women weren't allowed to serve in combat roles, so a lot of army jobs were off-limits. But there was a loophole. Women *could* be Black Hawk pilots in a war zone because this helicopter was mostly used in a support role. Tammy set her sights on flight school.

"I came sideways into aviation," she mused years later. The army, too. She never imagined that she would love it as much as she did. But there was another hurdle—getting into flight school was nearly impossible . . . *if* you were an active duty servicemember.

Tammy joined the reserves.

Reserves, National Guard, or Active Duty?

Unlike the full-time commitment of active duty, servicemembers in the US Army Reserve work in civilian jobs but are also part-time soldiers. They can be in the National Guard—often deployed by state governors to respond to state disasters—or in the regular reserves. While serving in this capacity, Reservists generally work one weekend a month, plus two weeks in the summer. Of course, a Reservist can be called up for temporary full-time duty, too, depending on the needs of the military. There are advantages to being a part-time versus a full-time servicemember. In the reserves, soldiers have the flexibility to maintain a civilian job. Additionally, while active duty soldiers frequently move every couple of years, Reservists can mostly live in one place and report to a nearby base for duty.

Tammy had to wait for an opening in flight school. When she finally got the call that there was a spot available, she dropped everything to drive 14 hours to Fort Rucker, Alabama, where the training would take place. Next she did everything she could to get assigned to the Black Hawk helicopter. It was going to be exceptionally difficult—only one Reservist out of the class of 40 would get that privilege. Tammy was determined it would be her.

"When the only obstacle is effort, then there is no obstacle, because I will move heaven and earth to get what I want, even if I have to do it one pebble at a time."

With this attitude, Tammy poured herself into studying and putting extra hours into practicing in a flight simulator. When she earned 100 percent on a systems test and came in first in her class in another section of the course, Tammy earned the right to fly the Black Hawk. Now she needed to figure out how.

Though she was always busy, learning to fly the Black Hawk was fun! Tammy loved every moment of flying the heavy bird. Then her year of flight school was up. Next came her first overseas assignment. She deployed to Egypt for a month to participate in a training exercise where she got to fly next to the pyramids. Other overseas deployments were just as thrilling. Tammy flew to the Amazon rainforest for a humanitarian mission called Operation New Horizon. Another mission was to clean up World War II debris from glaciers in Iceland.

The Black Hawk

The UH-60 Black Hawk (a utility helicopter) is named after a war leader of the Sauk Native American tribe born in 1767. The aircraft is mainly a support vehicle and troop carrier, though it can also be used for other missions such as medical evacuation, search and rescue, or armed escort. Weighing 22,000 pounds (10,000 kg), it is a powerful aircraft with two turboshaft engines and four blades. The Black Hawk crew consists of two pilots and one or two crew chiefs. The US Army has an inventory of over 2,000 of these multifunctional helicopters.

Aspects of Tammy's army training and later missions were challenging. But early on, Tammy had developed a strategy for coping when things got tough. Most things in life, she found, could be broken into smaller, manageable pieces. For instance, whenever she had to run, something she disliked as a child, she determined that if she could just make it to the next tree, she could then keep going, making a new target once she reached the first one.

Up until the attack, Tammy's deployment to Iraq had been relatively routine and often enjoyable. The combination of flying Black Hawks and the camaraderie of the other soldiers was something she cherished. Indeed, the people she worked with gave so much that she felt enormous respect and gratitude for being part of the army culture. Plus, each time she sat inside the helicopter's cockpit she knew she was doing something vital.

Just before the rocket strike, Tammy and the rest of the crew were flying fast and low, as per army protocol. Inside the cockpit, they were joking and enjoying themselves. At the first sound of bullets hitting the body of the helicopter, things turned instantly serious.

The attack and subsequent fight for survival changed Tammy in profound ways, and not just physically. At first she had to accept and live through nearly unbearable pain. Then, life as a double amputee was a new reality that required tough decisions and heartbreaking acceptance. At first Tammy was determined to continue flying, especially after she met another amputee who had been able to continue his piloting career. But Lieutenant Colonel Andrew Lourake had only lost one leg, and that one just above his knee. He was still capable of completing all the requirements of a mission. Tammy, unfortunately, learned that she was not. She would never fly for the army again.

While recovering at Walter Reed, patients often received messages or even visits from celebrities and government officials. One day, Illinois Senator Dick Durbin called to see if any wounded soldiers were well enough to attend the upcoming State of the Union Speech at the US Capitol as his guests. Though still weak and unable to sit up for more than 90 minutes, Tammy was set on going. She redoubled her efforts at recovery, and weeks later, she attended the event.

The chance encounter with Dick Durbin had a lasting impact on the direction of Tammy's life. During her 13-month recovery at Walter Reed, she had become an unofficial advocate for the wounded veterans there. After meeting the senator, Tammy began calling his office to bring up the problems and issues she was seeing. Eventually, he encouraged Tammy to run for office. Tammy was stunned. She had never considered becoming a politician. But then as she thought more about it, she realized that this was a direct way to help veterans. She began her campaign to win a seat in the House of Representatives—and lost.

It was a devastating loss, but Tammy didn't give up her mission to help veterans. She worked as director of the Illinois Department of Veterans' Affairs. Then, in 2008, Barack Obama offered her a job in his administration, still helping veterans. It was just a matter of time before she ran for Congress again. In 2012 Tammy ran for a seat in the House of Representatives, this time winning with over 20,000 votes. She served two terms before moving on to the Senate. While serving, she also gave birth to two precious daughters.

Today, Tammy Duckworth is Senator Duckworth. Her career has elevated her to heights she never could have fathomed as a child, allowing her to have direct influence over the lives of veterans. She attributes her success to hard work. "Hard work is my superpower," she admits. But it's more than this. Tammy holds deep a sense of grit and determination that pulled her from childhood poverty to a Black Hawk cockpit and finally to a seat in the US Senate. Above all, she cares fiercely for her family and for the men and women who so selflessly serve our country. Tammy also never takes anything for granted.

Every year on November 12, Tammy celebrates her "Alive Day." As she reflects on the circumstances that nearly conquered her, she repeats the warrior's ethos:

I will always place the mission first.

I will never accept defeat.

I will never quit . . .

Follow Tammy Duckworth Online

Website: www.duckworth.senate.gov

Instagram: @senduckworth

Twitter: @SenDuckworth

Facebook: Tammy Duckworth

Edgora McEwan: On the Rise

The alarm clock blinked 3:30 AM as it jarred Edgora McEwan awake. Her eyes popped open, and she smiled. No matter the dark hour—she was happy to get up and start her day. Today she was going to watch the sun rise over the desert. She would be doing it from the basket of a hot-air balloon.

The first thing Edgora did after she got up was check the weather report—again. Though heat was the one constant in the United Arab Emirates (U.A.E.), other environmental factors like wind or precipitation could drastically affect the flight. If conditions weren't optimal, today's hot-air balloon tour would be aborted. When she had last checked the forecast yesterday, it had called for excellent weather: no thunder clouds, high winds, or rain. Thankfully, circumstances hadn't changed. After fortifying herself with a quick cup of coffee and breakfast, Edgora headed to today's launch site.

For the past year, Edgora had been riding along with one of several hot-air balloon pilots so she could learn from experience. Someday, she vowed, she would earn her own pilot's license and become the first female in the U.A.E. to do so. But first she needed to learn everything there was to know about the sport. And there was a lot to learn.

Today, whether she got to fly was dependent not only on weather conditions, but also on how many people had shown up. With a maximum load of 24 passengers in the large capacity balloons, Edgora always hoped for a less than sold-out tour— or a no-show. She lucked out. There was space in the basket of today's hot-air balloon ride.

Even if there wasn't room for her that day, Edgora always helped the crew get things ready for the flight. The balloon itself—called the envelope—came in a giant stuff sack. The team spread out a huge tarp on the sand. Then they unfurled the massive fabric. Using a gas-powered fan, one person lifted the opening to the envelope so air could be directed inside. Initially, this air was not yet heated. Edgora was glad for the extra hours she spent at the gym. Setting up the balloon took a lot of muscle.

Once the envelope was sufficiently inflated, the next step was to turn on the propane burners. The flames would warm the air inside the envelope, allowing the balloon to lift off. Edgora monitored this next phase carefully. Without strict attention to the guidelines, the process could end in disaster. Today's ride would only be safe if the correct protocol was followed. Edgora mentally checked off the steps for ensuring safety:

Attach the basket securely to the envelope.

Position the burners exactly right.

Make sure the fuel lines are working properly.

The first step was perhaps the most obvious, but all were equally important. Despite the section of fire-resistant material surrounding the skirt of the envelope, the propane flames would, given the chance, easily burn the envelope if they weren't aimed correctly. Next, Edgora knew that if the fuel lines leaked or the air wasn't properly heated, the pilot could quickly lose control of the balloon.

Another danger could present itself once the envelope was even partially inflated with warm air. The threat of having the balloon drift away prematurely was one of the reasons the team started with the basket lying on its side. The ground crew also needed to tether the balloon or risk it floating away unmanned. Now Edgora double-checked the lines that anchored the aircraft to the heaviest object around, a nearby SUV. Everything was as it should be.

Edgora next helped turn on the three propane burners. She centered the nozzles so the flames would heat the air inside the envelope, a process that took several minutes. Once fully inflated, she helped tilt the basket upright. She looked over the equipment one last time. While it might seem to some people that a hot-air balloon ride is serene and peaceful, Edgora knew it took constant vigilance to keep things safe.

This morning, everything proceeded without a hitch. Edgora and the rest of the group were ready to go. She took a deep breath and grinned—no matter how many times she flew, there was always a familiar thrill that accompanied every hot-air balloon ride. She climbed into the rattan basket along with the pilot and today's passengers. With a nod to the pilot and ground crew, she disconnected the tethers. The balloon floated up, buoyed by the air and at the whim of the wind. Edgora was free.

How Does It Work?

A hot-air balloon operates because of the basic principle that warm air is less dense than cool air, and therefore rises. Science states that when air is heated within the balloon's envelope, it will achieve lift due to the denser, cooler atmosphere surrounding it. And though the concept of a hot-air balloon is relatively simple, the actual aircraft is complex. There are three main components: the basket, the burners, and the envelope. The basket is usually wicker, a style of construction that provides for a light but sturdy place to hold passengers, extra fuel tanks, and equipment. Some of the instruments on board include an altimeter to measure elevation, a rate of climb or descent indicator—a variometer—a fuel gauge, and a pyrometer, an instrument to measure the temperature inside the envelope. Next is the envelope, the usually tear-shaped component made up of long panels called gores that are sewn together. At the top of the envelope is a deflation port that can be controlled by the pilot. When she wants the balloon to descend, the pilot can open this seam and allow a portion of the warm air to exit, thus causing the balloon to lose altitude.

Edgora was born in Uzbekistan, a small landlocked country that was formerly part of the Soviet Union. She grew up with her mom and sister—her dad passed away when she was an infant.

From her earliest memories, Edgora was adventurous. She loved learning, too, and when she wasn't swimming, running, or exploring outside, she spent her time reading books. While she learned English by taking language classes after school, instruction in the school itself was in both Uzbek and Russian. She didn't know it then, but her fluency in different languages was going to be a useful skill during her piloting career. Passengers—and other pilots—came from all over the world.

The school system in Uzbekistan is different than in the United States. Edgora studied a compulsory curriculum until the ninth grade. Students were then given a choice. They could either begin college level courses that would help them transition to university later or they could take a vocational or technical selection of courses. Academically gifted, Edgora took the first option and graduated from high school ranking fifth in her class. Then she ran into an obstacle. She failed the entrance exams for university.

Edgora was mortified. Wasn't she always the one who did so well in school? Didn't she just graduate as one of the top performers in her class? While she wasn't going to give up her dream of going to college, Edgora needed to catch her breath and think about her next steps. She decided to visit an aunt and uncle who lived in Dubai in the U.A.E. *I'll stay for a year,* she told herself. *I'll do distance learning and then come back to take the exams again.*

Life in Dubai was hot and sandy and unlike anything Edgora had experienced before. It was also beautiful and full of new opportunities. Here, she took her first hot-air balloon ride. She recalls, "It was pure love from first sight. It was magical, like floating on a magic carpet." She studied the pilot as he monitored the burners to heat the air inside the balloon. She watched him guide the balloon according to the wind. She wondered, *Could I ever do that, too?* But was being a hot-air balloon pilot even possible for a woman in this country? No female in the U.A.E. had ever earned the certification necessary to pilot a hot-air balloon. The idea persisted, however, and Edgora looked into how to achieve her goal.

After riding along with other pilots for about a year to learn and fuel this new passion, Edgora located a training center in Italy where she could get a license to become a hot-air balloon pilot. There were challenges, though. For one, it was expensive. Then, money aside, she was going to have to leave her family to attend the course. She would be in a new country by herself with no guarantee of success. *Am I crazy for wanting this so much?* she asked herself.

No. Edgora decided that no matter what, she wanted—needed—to get this certification. She rented a room through Airbnb and booked a plane ticket to Mondovi, Italy. As she packed her suitcase, she told herself, *This is my moment. This is when my dream comes true.*

Earning a hot-air balloon license took dedication and lots of hard work. The first stage was mastering five theory exams. These were in navigation, aviation law, human performance, balloon systems, and meteorology. There was a lot to know, but Edgora was no stranger to hard work. She hit the books. The meteorology portion of the training was especially daunting. Because a balloon had no steering wheel or set of brakes, Edgora studied how a balloon's drift was entirely dependent on wind currents—and her ability to understand and use them. She needed to become an expert in monitoring and predicting what the local atmospheric conditions would do next.

Edgora studied the ideal situation for flying a hot-air balloon. This included good visibility, light winds, and no rain or other precipitation that could add weight to the balloon and damage it. She learned to identify wind patterns, including where there were downdrafts, warm or cold fronts forming, pressure systems, or other potentially hazardous conditions. She analyzed different cloud formations, a visual indicator of impending weather. As magical and peaceful as it was to fly in a hot-air balloon, Edgora knew that she would have to become an expert in all these details if she were to be trusted in the role of pilot.

A Sheep, a Duck, and a Rooster

It was the summer of 1783. Two brothers, Joseph-Michel and Jacques-Étienne Montgolfier, had invented the first practical hot-air balloon. It started when they made the connection that smoke rises and that it might therefore have lifting power. If they could capture enough hot smoke in a cloth or paper bag, would it be able to raise the bag into the air? It would.

After experimenting with a homemade, toy-sized balloon, the brothers constructed a larger balloon, this one made from taffeta material and lined with paper. They conducted a public demonstration on June 4, 1783. Fueled by a fire made from damp straw and wool, their bulb-shaped balloon floated up an estimated 6,000 feet and drifted for about a mile. This attracted the attention of several powerful people including the king of France, Louis XVI.

The brothers prepared another demonstration. This

time, they placed three animals in a basket under their balloon—a sheep, a duck, and a rooster. They wanted to see if the animals would survive the unknown conditions high above the Earth's surface. They did. After an eight-minute flight, the creatures landed unharmed.

Before Edgora was allowed to fly solo, she had to build up 16 hours of supervised flight time with an instructor. In addition to the theory portion of the course that she had committed to memory, she trained herself to have situational awareness. What obstacles were around her? What power lines, trees, church steeples, smokestacks, towers, or natural formations was she going to have to avoid? How could she use the wind current to help her get where she wanted to go?

Each time she ascended with her instructor, Edgora refined her ability to manage the balloon alone. Finally, the day came for her check flight. She would go up with a flight examiner who would assess her ability to handle herself and the balloon. If she passed the test, the next step would be to go solo. Then, if all went well again, she would earn her private pilot's license in hot-air ballooning.

Not surprisingly, Edgora did well on her check flight. Now she was one step away from earning her certification—the solo flight.

After a few cancelled flights due to weather, it was finally time for Edgora to fly alone. She arrived at the launch site early and put on a pair of protective gloves. Things *looked* the same at the site, but today everything would be entirely different. No one but Edgora would stand in the balloon's basket, monitoring the instruments and determining the best course. It was up to her—and the wind—to decide what happened and where she would land.

Up, Up, and Away: Steering a Hot-Air Balloon

The pilot's main means of control is by moving the balloon up and down. By turning on the propane burners, she can heat the air inside the balloon even further, making it even less dense and thus causing it to rise. A small valve in the crown of the balloon has a rope attached. When the pilot opens this valve, some of the warmer air can be released, causing the balloon to descend.

Horizontal movement and speed are less precise. An experienced pilot works in tandem with the wind. She can position the balloon to catch various wind currents, which will, in turn, determine the speed and forward movement. For this reason, a balloonist doesn't know precisely where she will land and carries a phone or radio to remain in contact with her ground crew. They will follow in a vehicle and get as close to the landing site as possible.

As Edgora worked beside the others for the preflight inspection and briefing, she didn't have time to dwell on the momentous occasion. Then she was standing in the basket—alone—and giving a thumbs-up to the ground crew. She opened the burners and dropped the tether. She was away!

With her landing spot predetermined, Edgora now concentrated on the flight. Since she was flying low, she had the ground in clear focus. She sailed over vineyards and fields. She saw deer and waved to people below her. Cars honked their horns for her. It was exhilarating. A peace and sense of accomplishment washed over her as she floated on the perfect air.

A short 45 minutes later, it was over. Edgora knew, however, that the experience had changed her. It had been risky, sure, but not much more than getting in a car every day. Besides, she knew she could do it. She had checked—and rechecked—each aspect of how to ensure a safe flight. Now she was qualified to float like a cloud as a hot-air balloon pilot.

Later, Edgora thought about all she had accomplished. "To be able to fly this wonderful aircraft was magnificent. Exploring the beautiful scenery from above and finally being able to do that on my own was priceless."

Back in the U.A.E., Edgora made headlines. She was the country's first female hot-air balloon pilot. She reflected on her life and how the failed university entrance exam had led to her life in this new country, how a spur-of-the-moment balloon ride had resulted in her earning this distinction. It started with that spark of interest followed by lots of determination and hard work. "Passion and love take over," she muses. No matter the multitude of tests, no matter the hours in the gym to build up muscle, for Edgora, flying a balloon is as close to perfect as one can get.

Follow Edgora McEwan Online

Instagram: @edgora.in.dubai

Facebook: Edgora Mambetalieva

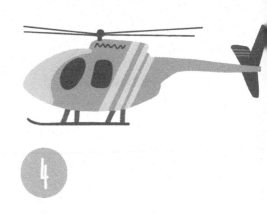

4

Dede Murawsky:
Horseback to Medevac

Like many people, Dede Murawsky wasn't sure what she wanted to be when she grew up. She was interested in college but didn't want to spend money she didn't have on an aimless goal. She was passionate about the horses on her family's farm, but that wasn't a career path. Then, one day her best friend's dad bought an ultralight aircraft. When Mr. Stockton offered Dede a ride, her vision for what she wanted to do after high school became a little clearer.

The aircraft was small, no more than a few hundred pounds. It was open to the air, a two-seater with a high wing that you could manipulate using a steering bar in the front. There was a small engine attached to the back. Dede adjusted her helmet while Mr. Stockton checked over the aircraft. Was there enough fuel? Were the wings attached securely? Was the engine running properly? It was a perfect day for the flight, sunny and not too much wind. As Dede buckled into a sturdy harness under a web of poles and wires, she didn't see how the seemingly flimsy craft could possibly lift them into the air.

The tiny vehicle raced down the runway at Herlong Recreational Airport near Jacksonville, Florida, and tottered into the air. Once airborne, the ultralight climbed higher. A few hundred feet from the ground, Dede had a bird's-eye view of the airport. She realized that what she had assumed were extra-large storage sheds were actually hangers for a whole community of small plane owners that she'd never known existed. Her heart flooded with fascination and joy as they flew over a golf course and then over her house. Dede was sad when the flight came to an end.

"It was pure amazement and the freest I had ever felt."

The experience had piqued an enchantment with airplanes. How could Dede find out more? Where could she learn to fly? Shortly after the experience, an army recruiter visited her high school, and Dede saw her path forward.

Dreams of Flying

As long as humans have watched birds in flight, they have dreamed of soaring through the air themselves. In 1485 Leonardo da Vinci sketched his famous "ornithopter," an early step in the development of the helicopter. Over his lifetime, he created over 100 drawings to demonstrate the feasibility of human flight. Those who followed referred to his and others' designs and put theory into practice. Sir George Cayley is credited with building the first successfully manned glider. Otto Lilienthal, an engineer from Germany, advanced wing designs and performed nearly 2,000 glider flights before fatally crashing. Finally, two Ohio brothers achieved a stupendous milestone—they flew the first engine-powered plane. On December 17, 1903, Orville and Wilbur Wright took turns flying their invention and ultimately achieved a flight of 59 seconds and 852 feet. Their success opened the way for the aviation industry.

Dede grew up on a horse farm in the middle of Florida. She is the oldest sibling and spent her childhood with the two brothers who came next. She helped with farm chores and joined 4-H, a youth organization that encourages hands-on experiences and leadership opportunities. With the club's guidance, one year Dede raised a pig. She also participated in horse shows. A decent athlete, Dede played soccer and enjoyed it, though it wasn't her passion. What she loved the most was competitive trail riding. Many weekends were spent riding up to 25 miles in the woods. If it was a two-day tournament, she might ride twice that far.

When Dede fell in love with airplanes, it was a shift from everything she knew and what she'd grown up doing. Still, maybe it was her familiarity and comfort around horses that had helped awaken her desire to become a pilot—later in life she reflected that a lot of the pilots she knew had close ties to horses. Perhaps it was the adrenaline rush of galloping on a formidable creature many times her weight. Maybe it was the speed or the feeling of eating up miles powered by something other than her own legs. One thing was for sure: Dede suddenly knew what she wanted. The day she walked into the military recruitment office, she told the recruiter, "I want a job that puts me around airplanes."

Dede enlisted in the air force, an experience that would challenge her physically and mentally. That September, after she graduated from high school, she flew to Lackland Air Force Base in San Antonio, Texas, where she began her military career with Basic Training. The pace was intense, and she seemed to be always exhausted or hungry. In addition to fitness drills and hands-on practice with weapons and equipment, there were classroom lessons, too. Dede studied topics such as air force history, military protocol, and how to be a good airman. She enjoyed the classes and wanted to retain everything she was learning, but with the exertion of everything else she was doing, it was a struggle to keep her eyes open.

Finally, Basic Training was over, and Dede was now an airman. Next up was technical school, this time for nine months at Keesler Air Force Base in Biloxi, Mississippi. This training would prepare her for a specific job within the air force.

Though Dede learned valuable skills to help her support various air operations, she still wasn't a pilot.

Dede waited to find out where she would be stationed next. Lucky for her, it was in Hawaii, at Wheeler Army Airfield with the 25th Air Support Operations Squadron. There she got her first helicopter ride while doing a joint training exercise with a group of marines. The CH-46, a large cargo helicopter, picked up Dede and the others from her squadron. They filed inside and sat along the wall of the helicopter. A few minutes into the flight, one of the crew chiefs pointed at Dede. Did she want to tour the helicopter?

Dede attached a "monkey harness," a safety tether that clipped into the floor. Now she could walk around, look over the pilots' shoulders into the cockpit, and lean out the gunner window. Looking over the magnificent Pacific Ocean from a few hundred feet up was a defining moment. How could she fulfill her dream of becoming a pilot?

At the time, Dede's job brought her around planes, but it seemed doubtful that she'd ever be able to fly one. Most future pilots were Air Force Academy graduates, not enlisted airmen. Even then, they had to have exceptionally high grades to stand out in the hypercompetitive field. Dede had done well, but she didn't have that same edge. Sure, it was possible to stay with the air force and hope that in a few years she might end up as a pilot, but that path was uncertain. Fortunately, she found a better way.

Dede was used to training with soldiers from different branches of the military. One day, when she happened to meet some army helicopter pilots, she realized *I can do that.* Dede made a decision: she transitioned from the air force to the army and traveled to Fort Rucker, Alabama, to attend Warrant Officer Candidate School, a course designed to create technical officers from the pool of enlisted soldiers. Dede followed this with a grueling three weeks of Survival, Evasion, Resistance, Escape (SERE) school. If Dede was going to be a pilot in a war zone, she would need to understand how to survive if her aircraft ever went down in hostile territory. Finally, she was ready for flight school. Dede was going to learn how to fly a helicopter.

The Fort Rucker training facility felt like it was in the middle of nowhere. The stage fields had several lanes of runways, and multiple pilots-in-training were practicing at the same time. Dede started in a training helicopter, a small, two-seat aircraft. Her instructor was an older man, a Vietnam veteran who obviously loved what he was doing. He was also strict—there was no room for incompetence. Dede learned the basics. Then she became an expert.

For the final segment of the training, Dede studied the tactical aspects of flying a combat helicopter. Next she narrowed her focus to the Kiowa Warrior. This single-engine aircraft was used mostly to conduct aerial surveillance and to support soldiers on the ground. It had a high-tech scouting device mounted on top that included cameras, thermal imaging equipment, and a laser range finder to help determine the distance to an object. The helicopter was also armed with weapons.

The Kiowa was designed for two crewmembers, and because of the equipment onboard, it was capable of using thermal imaging to see into the dark. Dede racked up hundreds of flight hours, flying day and night training missions as well as cross-country flights. As cool as it was to simply fly such an amazing aircraft, Dede kept her eye on the real purpose of the rigorous training. Some day she might provide tangible—even life or death—support to troops on the ground. Everything she did was in preparation for potentially going overseas.

Dede soon had her chance. She deployed to Afghanistan. For the months-long assignment, she ate, slept, and breathed helicopters. She lived in close quarters with the other pilots, and aside from one other woman, they were all men. Dede now put all her training into practice. Her missions included convoy security, reconnaissance, or escorting Black Hawk or Chinook helicopters. She also helped provide "eyes in the air" to ground troops. From above, she could see where the soldiers were headed. Were there any ambushes set up ahead? Was there any danger that was invisible to those on the ground? If there *was* an immediate threat, the helicopter Dede flew packed some smaller ammunition, enough to hold off the enemy until a more powerful aircraft could come along. It was a crucial and necessary job, and Dede was happy to protect the vulnerable soldiers on the ground. She didn't feel nervous or afraid. For one, there was so much to do that there wasn't time for her to feel stressed. Plus, she knew she was a lot safer than those traveling by land.

Dede completed a second similar deployment. After both tours were over, the army stopped using the Kiowa helicopter. Rather than train on something new, she decided to leave the military and get a job in the civilian world. She considered two avenues: working in the oil fields or flying a medevac helicopter. She applied and was soon offered a job as a medevac helicopter pilot.

Help Wanted: Helicopter Pilot

Outside of the military, licensed helicopter pilots have a variety of job options open to them. For one, companies hire commercial pilots for the tourist industry. Pilots might fly sightseeing tours or transport heli-skiers to pristine backcountry locations. Emergency services such as fire, medical, and law enforcement use helicopters to fight fires, transport patients, patrol highways, or conduct search and rescue operations. News outlets use helicopters to get to a scene quickly. This versatile craft is even used to herd livestock, a sometimes quicker and more efficient method than using horses. Offshore oil platforms rely on helicopters to transport personnel and supplies back and forth. These jobs all have one thing in common: the pilot is responsible for the safety of all passengers and equipment onboard.

Today, Dede loves her job flying an H-130 medical transport helicopter. She's making a real difference, often literally helping to save peoples' lives. Similar to a firefighter or emergency medical technician (EMT), Dede and her team wait for distress calls to come into the center. Some days the red phone designated for the purpose of relaying emergencies hardly rings; other days it can be ringing constantly. As a pilot, it's Dede's job to answer the call and determine if the team can accept the request. If so, Dede, along with a nurse and paramedic, will fly to the scene.

There are two types of calls. One is for a medical transport. Here, a patient who is in stable condition needs to be moved to a different hospital or facility. The other circumstance is when there has been an accident and immediate air transport has been requested.

Dede works 12-hour shifts. These alternate between days and nights. She works one week on and one week off. In a month, she'll have two weeks of day shifts. The next month she'll have two weeks of nights. While at work, everyone has their own room and, if not busy, Dede tries to take short naps. In the facility there is also a gym and kitchen. But while there can be downtime, Dede knows she has to be ready at a moment's notice. Once the red phone rings, every minute extra can mean the difference between someone's life or death. Her only focus then must be on the mission.

Prior to receiving an emergency call, Dede makes sure everything is ready to go. She always keeps her boots on. She eats when she's hungry. She looks over the helicopter to make sure the maintenance is complete. Are the fluid levels good? Is there enough fuel, and has she taken a fuel sample to make sure no water or contaminants have gotten in? Is the helicopter in peak condition? Next, Dede keeps on top of the weather. What is the forecast for their service area? What does she need to know about wind, fog, cloud cover, or rain if they are asked to fly out?

When a dispatcher calls, Dede assesses the request and must decide if it's within regulations. She gets as much information as she can, so she can brief the nurse and paramedic while they take a moment to prepare. While Dede plans how they'll get there, the nurse grabs fresh blood from the fridge. The rest of the trauma equipment is already packed on the helicopter. Dede does a final assessment of weather and the route. She analyzes the obstacles along the helicopter's flight, especially power lines and towers or tall buildings. Though the FAA discourages rushing through the preflight safety checks and preparation, Dede's team generally arrives on the scene in less than 10 minutes.

In the Helicopter Pilot Seat

While women make up a tiny fraction of all US helicopter pilots today, studies show that females make excellent pilots. There is a unique skill set to flying this type of aircraft. Along with good coordination and excellent eyesight and hearing, pilots need to be able to handle a number of complex tasks all at once. Pilots must be patient, calm, and always professional. Equally important, a helicopter pilot is someone who doesn't panic or crack under pressure. She must be able to think rationally, despite any emergency that pops up. Many women are great at these skills. Today, several organizations encourage females to pursue a career in aviation. Some of these are *Whirly-Girls*, *Women in Aviation*, and *Girls with Wings*.

Once on the ground, it's the nurse and paramedic's job to take care of the patient. Since Dede is the only person who can fly the helicopter, she stays in the background. If the others are too busy, she tries to get any relevant information from the police officers who are already at the scene of the accident. She can brief the nurse and paramedic once inbound to the nearest hospital. It's a highly organized team effort that literally saves lives.

Dede muses on the twisted path she took to get to where she is today. Unlike friends who went to college with a specific job in mind, Dede's career has taken many turns. While she knew early on that she wanted to be a pilot, it was a series of little steps and embracing new opportunities that led her to the job she holds today. She worked hard, studying and persevering as she figured out where she would go next. Who knew that her first ride in that ultralight plane would lead to a career in flying?

For Dede, as long as she can serve others in the pilot seat of a helicopter, she knows she is exactly where she needs to be.

Follow Dede Murawsky Online

Website: https://quickwhittravel.com/2020/09/28/fly-like
-a-girl-what-its-like-to-be-a-woman-medevac-helicopter
-pilot/

Instagram: @dedemsky

Anne Macdonald: A Rank Above

Anne Macdonald slipped into one of two seats in the bubble-shaped cockpit of the orange training helicopter. Her instructor, Buddy Bishop, sat in the other. She grasped the cyclic with her right hand, the lever that caused the aircraft to tilt forward, rearward, or move to either side. Her left hand was on the collective, which controlled raising or lowering the helicopter. The throttle, regulating speed, was located here as well. Finally, two pedals on the floor were for maintaining direction or aircraft heading. Flying the helicopter was the ultimate exercise in being able to multitask.

"Hatch Tower, this is Army 236, Runway 2, ready for take-off . . ." Anne radioed the ground crew using the specific aviation jargon that left no room for misinterpretation.

Anne practiced maneuvering, including hovering in place. *Gentle, gentle,* she reminded herself. This was the hardest move to master, requiring a delicate manipulation of the controls. At first, the helicopter veered to the right, then left. Finally, she exerted just the right amount of pressure.

"You found the hover button," Mr. Bishop told her. He meant that Anne had mastered one of the necessary skills to fly solo. *Yes!* Anne's excitement evaporated when he added, "But you're not ready to fly alone yet."

Crushed, Anne reflected on her performance, dissecting how she had handled each maneuver. *What am I doing wrong?* she asked herself. *Why doesn't he think I'm ready?*

The next day was Anne's birthday. As usual, she took off in the helicopter with Mr. Bishop. Shortly into the flight, he took control of the throttle and deliberately over-sped the engine, pushing the aircraft to its outer limit. The helicopter yawed violently to the right, and it was up to Anne to bring it back under control. She handled the potential emergency competently but was more than a little irritated. When they landed, she turned to him and demanded, "Why'd you do that?"

"You need to be ready for anything," Mr. Bishop told her. How would Anne react if something out of the ordinary occurred? Next, he took his cap from his pocket, and, taking a large clip, he attached it to a spot in the cockpit. "Take care of this hat," he told her. He unstrapped his seat harness and stepped out of the helicopter. Anne *was* ready to go solo—Mr. Bishop had intentionally planned it so it would coincide with her birthday.

Nervous, but confident she could do it, Anne glanced at the empty seat beside her. Her first task was to inform the people in the control tower that she was flying alone. She spoke into the radio, her voice high-pitched and fast. By her third pass over the field, her voice—and her heart—had settled. She had this. She knew what she was doing.

Finally, elated, Anne set the aircraft on the tarmac and shut it down. *And I get paid for this!* She unbuckled and stepped away from the helicopter.

Whoosh! Her classmates came over with trashcans of water and dumped them over Anne. It was a good-natured aviators' tradition—whenever someone flew alone for the first time, she was doused with water. Mr. Bishop handed her a certificate to commemorate the event.

Anne looked around. Everything suddenly seemed more vivid, the sky the bluest blue, the grass the greenest green. *What a thrill! This is freedom,* she mused. She couldn't stop smiling.

Pigeons and Angels

The language of aviation is unique and specific. Communicating clearly has high stakes. Second-guessing a crewmember's meaning can lead to accidents, or worse. Aviators use a phonetic alphabet. For example, *alpha, bravo,* or *charlie* for A, B, or C are used to avoid misunderstanding. Numbers have unmistakable names, too. *Tree* is used for *three*, and *niner* instead of *nine*. Distinct terms identify various situations. *Pigeons* refers to the aircraft's heading or magnetic bearing. *Angels* refers to altitude. A *bandit* is an identified enemy aircraft, while a *bogey* is an unknown one. Whenever a crewmember radios the ground support, they must identify themselves with a call sign. For example, they might begin a transmission with "This is Freedom's Eagle Six."

Growing up, Anne was no stranger to the military. She was what some people affectionately call an "army brat," a child whose parent or parents are career military. Her father was an officer in the army and, except for a year when he was stationed in Vietnam, wherever his job took him, the family went too. Anne was born in Germany, but the family quickly moved to Texas, Pennsylvania, and Virginia before heading back to Europe. This time, the family traveled aboard a steamship to Bremerhaven, a US Army base in Germany.

Living in Germany was a new experience, but sobering, too. It was the height of the Cold War, a period of tension between the United States and the Soviet Union. To Anne, living there was eye-opening, especially when she and her sisters took a train to Berlin. The Berlin Wall was still in place—a fortified barrier between democratic West Berlin and the Soviet-controlled part of the city. Anne noted the damage caused by bullets and mortars, a sharp reminder of World War II. The experience further instilled a sense of service in Anne. She cherished the values of her country and knew that someday, when she grew up, she wanted to somehow give back.

Her family's frequent moves made Anne resilient and self-reliant. She learned to quickly make new friends and adapt to new situations. When her family relocated back to the United States, she completed high school on base at Fort Knox, an army post in Kentucky. Living there further ingrained in Anne the importance and honor of serving in the military. When the cannon sounded every evening at five o'clock to signal the end of the duty day, soldiers respected the flag by stopping to salute while civilians placed a hand over their heart. It was a daily reminder of the sacrifice servicemembers and their families give to the country. Fort Knox was also where Anne first thought about becoming an aviator.

Anne's best friend at Fort Knox was the daughter of squadron commander, Lieutenant Colonel Roy Wulff. One day, he told the girls, "I'm getting two women in my squadron. They're in flight school now." He followed with a casual comment that would have a lasting impact on Anne. "You could do that, too."

By now, Anne knew she wanted to go to college, but it wasn't until her senior year that the decision of where became clear. It was 1975, and for the first time in history, the US Military Academy—commonly referred to as West Point—was opening its doors to women the following school year. Anne had no idea about this until a liaison officer from West Point came to her high school. Her guidance counselor urged Anne to apply. *I'm not sure I can do it*, she questioned herself. *Okay, just fill the application out. Just do it.* She decided she had to at least try.

Several weeks later Anne came home to find her sisters playing on the lawn. The governor of Kentucky had called, they told her. She was going to West Point!

Anne knew she needed to focus. Could she handle the same academic, physical, and mental challenges as her male counterparts? She'd always done well in school and knew how to study, but what about the physical requirements? She *thought* she was tough enough . . . she was healthy and active in a variety of sports. She was a strong swimmer. She knew she wanted to serve her country. But opening West Point to women was a huge change. How would the men react?

Footprints in the Snow

West Point is located north of New York City. Winters are cold, with the average snowfall in January being about 12 inches. Like footprints in the snow, the first women to enter West Point had to mark the way for those who came later. It wasn't easy. Out of the 119 women who gave their oath to "duty, honor, and country" during the institution's reception ceremony on July 7, 1976, only 62 graduated four years later. From the beginning, female cadets were followed, sometimes hounded, by news journalists. For the most part, the women didn't want the extra attention. It was hard enough to be the first to lay a path for other women to follow. But when President Ford signed Public Law 94-106, allowing women to attend the previously all-male military colleges, women finally became part of "The Long, Gray Line." They were graduates of the United States' premier military academy.

Not surprisingly, West Point *was* challenging. For one thing, not everyone was on board with the decision to include women. Some of the male classmates were rude, while others were downright hostile. Some of them asked Anne, "What are you doing here?" Or, "Don't you know that this is no place for a woman?"

Then there was the physical difficulty of passing the same standards as the men. Initially, running in formation was tough. Anne hadn't done a lot of running in high school, and, especially carrying a heavy rucksack, it was grueling. The thought of quitting flashed through her mind.

Anne called home one day when she was feeling especially low. Her mother told her, "Anne, if they're *really* doing that to you, then you should come home." Her implication was: *Think about what you're saying. Reassess the environment by seeing past your emotions and viewing the situation realistically.*

"Maybe I'll try one more day."

Life at West Point didn't become any less challenging, but as Anne got better at the physical and mental tasks, she felt a deep sense of accomplishment and purpose. While it was true that they did "more before 9:00 AM than most people do all day," the hectic pace of each day instilled in her a powerful discipline that she knew had changed her forever. Then, suddenly it seemed, it was graduation day.

Early Wednesday morning on May 28, 1980, was sunny and already getting warm. Anne stood outside the cadet chapel on campus, reflecting on what a monumental day it was for the 178-year-old institution. In a few minutes Anne would join the other 6.7 percent of the graduating class who were women. She felt proud to be a part of them—and an enormous responsibility for those who would follow.

Anne adjusted her officer's cap, part of the full-dress regalia she was wearing for the ceremony. She knew she looked sharp. Every "bullet button" on her embroidered gray jacket shone in the sun. The buckle on the sash across her chest was a polished gold. West Point was rich in tradition, and today's elaborate uniform was just one thing that set it apart from other colleges. Anne marched with her class into Michie Stadium, humbled by the opportunity she'd been given—and thankful that she had measured up. She scanned the stands, hoping to catch sight of her family.

When the first female cadet, Andrea Hollen, went to the stage to receive her diploma, Anne felt a thrill run through her. It hadn't been easy to be the first class of female cadets, but today there was a resounding feeling of rightness. Women *could* do this—the last four years were proof of that.

"Class dismissed."

Anne tossed her cap into the air with the rest of her classmates. As she hugged those around her, she felt the magnitude of her—and their—accomplishment. But really, life was just beginning. Anne had been selected for a coveted spot in flight school, and after that, who knew what would happen? One thing *was* clear. The army had a new slogan, "Be all you can be," and Anne was determined to embrace that challenge.

Of the dozens of other women in Anne's class, only three would go to flight school, and just 10 percent of the overall class would attend. Anne knew it was a privilege and an honor to have earned a the opportunity. Besides, it sounded fun to fly a helicopter. She couldn't wait!

Flight school took place at Fort Rucker, Alabama. There were four main phases to the course: basic flight concepts, primary, instruments, and combat skills. At first, Anne and the other students studied in the classroom. They learned the basics of aerodynamics, weather, and how to communicate properly. Then they headed to Hatch Stagefield to practice in a training helicopter, the TH-55.

The next sections of the course involved a UH-1, a larger utility helicopter. Anne studied flight rules and learned to use all the instruments onboard. She started in the UH-1 flight simulator, but once proficient, she moved onto the actual aircraft. She became an expert on reading maps and understanding navigation. She flew at night using night goggles to see. Cockpit management meant understanding aircraft systems and their status. How much fuel was left? What weapons were onboard? Who was doing what task? Anne practiced the procedures hundreds of times until her reactions were automatic. One saying etched itself into her head: "take-off is optional; landing is mandatory."

Anne graduated nine months later. With her shiny aviation wings pinned to her uniform, she could not have been prouder or happier. Now it was time to put her new skills to use.

Slower and Lower

Helicopters have several advantages over fixed wing aircraft. For one, helicopters can go into remote regions where airplanes can't. Since they don't require a runway, helicopters can land in any flat, open space. This type of aircraft can also fly in congested areas and lower in altitude. In mountainous regions, a helicopter has a huge advantage over a plane. It can maneuver over mountain ranges and transport troops and supplies to isolated locations otherwise reachable only by ground transportation or foot. Some models function as an aerial ambulance (medevac) with space to carry wounded personnel.

Several army helicopters are also used for defense—they are outfitted with weapons and can provide self-defense and security to those on the ground.

When Anne graduated from flight school, laws at the time prevented females from flying in direct combat—though in reality, plenty of women found themselves in harm's way. Anne's first assignment was with the 128th Aviation Company at Camp Page in South Korea. The US base was 35 miles south of the demilitarized zone that separated the country from North Korea. Her job there, a hectic six days a week, included leadership duties such as overseeing refueling efforts and maintenance logistics and tracking aircraft. As an army aviator and an officer, she still flew, but not every day.

When Anne did fly, it was frequently for a "tech supply and oil run," a mission to bring supplies and equipment to servicemembers stationed at various remote locations. Each flight required extensive preparation. Anne helped physically check that all components of the helicopter were working well. In the winter in South Korea, this task required her to withstand the bitter cold. Though Anne could usually go inside to warm up after this duty, one time she didn't have that luxury.

The mission that day was to fly to the top of a mountain where a US radio installation had been set up, crewed by a small group of servicemembers. Immediately after the preflight checks, Anne climbed into the cockpit, her hands numb from the cold. It was an effort to make them function properly, and they ached when they finally began to thaw.

Flying to the remote location required specific procedures. It would take extra fuel, for one, and with strong winds and the high altitude, it could be a treacherous flight. Knowing this, the men at the station were exceptionally grateful for the mail and fresh supplies. Anne knew she was making a difference.

After her tour in South Korea, the army stationed Anne all over the globe, first back to the States and then to Germany, the Middle East, and again to South Korea. For every assignment, her leadership skills improved—and her superiors took note. Anne rose in rank, each time earning more and more responsibility. She deployed twice to the Middle East, a sobering experience that was much more real than the two-dimensional news clips she'd seen on TV. As she flew over destroyed tanks and vast stretches of concertina wire, a line from the national anthem played over in her head, *And the rocket's red glare, the bombs bursting in air.* More than ever, Anne felt the weight of duty and the honor of service.

Next, Anne was stationed in Afghanistan to support the mission Operation Enduring Freedom. By now she had been promoted to brigadier general, the second female from West Point to have earned this elevated rank. Her position in the country was Deputy Commanding General for Police Development. The mission was a cooperative, international endeavor through NATO—the North Atlantic Treaty Organization. She was there to help train Afghan men and women to be police officers. When Anne was invited to the oath ceremony for the first female class in the Afghan National Army Officer Candidate School, she reflected on her own reception ceremony at West Point.

"Here we are, 34 years later, in Afghanistan, and these women, these brave women, are doing exactly the same thing we did." It was a poignant reminder of the magnitude of Anne's accomplishments—and those of the Afghan women.

Today, though Anne has retired from the military, she continues to mentor young people and share her knowledge. Not only has Anne achieved incredible personal success, but she also continues to help lay the trail for others. *Footprints in the snow . . .*

Follow Anne Macdonald Online

Website: https://www.awfdn.org/leadership/anne-f-macdonald/

Part II
Altitude

(30,000—45,000 Feet)

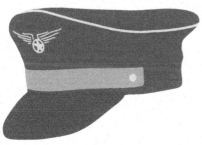

Tammie Jo Shults: Flying Past the Noes

"Girls don't fly for a living."

It was career day, and Tammie Jo Shults was one of the seniors who had bussed in from neighboring Tularosa High School, New Mexico. The bus had arrived late, so Tammie Jo scooted into the classroom where everyone else was already seated. The session was about aviation, led by an air force colonel. He turned to Tammie Jo and asked if she was lost. He added, "This is career day, not hobby day."

Despite her embarrassment and the man's obvious disapproval that she was female, Tammie Jo stayed to hear his lecture. She was mesmerized. Being a pilot was *exactly* what she wanted to do with her life. But . . . was it even possible for a girl?

Tammie Jo went to talk to her guidance counselor. There she received her second "no." That career choice was out of reach, the counselor told her. Tammie Jo needed to find something more practical, something realistic that she could actually accomplish.

Tammie Jo put aside the idea of being a pilot, but she didn't completely extinguish it. Burning quietly inside her, the idea of someday flying lay dormant for the next couple of years.

It didn't take much for Tammie Jo's hope to reignite. One day when she was in her senior year of college, she happened to meet a female air force pilot. Resurrecting her dream of becoming a pilot herself, she stopped at a local air force recruitment office.

"No," the recruiter told her politely when Tammie Jo asked if she could apply.

She went to a different recruiter. "No." His answer was just as firm.

Well, what about the army? They have pilots, too, Tammie Jo thought. "No," came the answer again.

She tried the navy next after learning that in addition to ships, they also had a fleet of planes. This time the recruiter allowed her to take the military entrance exam called the Armed Services Vocational Aptitude Battery (ASVAB). She missed passing by six questions, but that didn't deter Tammie Jo. She would simply study and try again. Her second attempt six months later was much better. She was ecstatic with her successful score—until her hopes were smothered again. This time when she went to process her paperwork, a different recruiter refused to advance her application to the next step. It seemed like this was the final "no."

One day Tammie Jo was passing through Albuquerque, and she decided to give her dream one last shot. She called a new navy recruiter. He looked up her results on the ASVAB and told her to stop by. He processed her papers and within weeks, Tammie Jo's application was accepted.

She had gotten her first "yes."

Unrestricted

The final hurdle blocking women from serving in all specialty areas of the US military was lifted on Jan. 1, 2016. Before that time, certain fields were off-limits to women, including direct ground combat. In 1973 the US Navy was the first branch of the military to open flight school to women, and eight women were accepted into the program. Six of these women earned their wings—the certification to fly naval aircraft. The US Army followed with female helicopter pilots. In 1976 the US Air Force accepted female applicants, but it wasn't until 1993 that women were permitted to train in combat aircraft. Today there are no gender restrictions in the US military. Any qualified person who meets the standard can apply to become a pilot.

Tammie Jo describes her childhood as idyllic. She had been raised on a ranch where, out of necessity, everyone was assigned chores. From the time she was young, Tammie Jo had helped her family run the farm, including physical tasks like loading heavy bales of hay or spreading manure in the garden. Her family was close, and, though finances were usually tight and there was plenty of hard work, life on a farm was an adventure. This wasn't always the case at school. Tammie Jo's sister, Sandra, was a special needs child who struggled at a public school with people who often didn't understand her disabilities. It didn't take long for the bullies to target her. One day the bullying came to a head, and Tammie Jo decided to stop it.

A boy had just pushed Sandra under a parked school bus, dirtying her dress and scraping her skin. Tammie Jo checked to make sure her sister was okay. Then she climbed onto the bus and walked straight to the back where the bully was sitting. She drew her arm back—and walloped him. The boy didn't pick on Sandra again, and Tammie Jo learned a valuable lesson: she vowed to never let a bully win.

Tammie Jo's family had moved a couple of times. Now they lived on a farm near Holloman Air Force Base near Alamogordo, New Mexico. Aircraft training maneuvers happened over their home nearly daily. As Tammie Jo tilted her head skyward to watch the simulated dogfights in the air above her, she dreamed of becoming an air force pilot herself. She hurried to share her goal with her family. Her mom wasn't overly enthusiastic about the plan. Tammie Jo tried talking to her dad next. He suggested that she talk to an actual pilot to find out more.

Okay then . . . It's not a no, she told herself.

Tammie Jo set her sights on a career in aviation. But then, after being told that being a pilot was out of reach by both the air force colonel and her guidance counselor, she decided to study to become a veterinarian instead. After all, she loved animals, and on the farm, she'd learned how to take care of them. She put her new plan into action.

Tammie Jo and her older brother, Dwight, took on extra jobs so they could save enough money to go to college. She completed high school and, four years later, graduated not as a veterinarian, but with degrees in biology and agribusiness— another detour from her dream.

Finally, though, Tammie Jo had her chance to join the military. When she graduated from the US Navy on June 21, 1985, she was as an ensign, a junior grade commissioned officer. Next up was flight school at the Naval Air Station in Corpus Christi, Texas.

Flight training was busy—and intense. It seemed like there was more book work than there was actual flying. This was good, though. The instructors wanted to make sure that every student aviator knew *exactly* what to do. This was especially critical during the out of control flight training (OCF) section of the course.

Controlling the Out of Control

As part of flight school, all student aviators are put through a series of out of control flights (OCF). Here, an instructor introduces a number of non-standard maneuvers such as stalls and spins. This phase is called the departure—the period when the plane goes from a controlled to an uncontrolled flight. The student pilot must recognize the problem and recover from each event using techniques specific to the situation. It can be a nerve-wracking and disorienting experience. The key is to maintain calm and rely on the instruments inside the plane rather than human perception, which can often provide erroneous information. At an altitude of 5,000 feet, if the pilots are unable to stabilize the plane, they must bail out and parachute to safety.

"You're cleared to fly."

Tammie Jo had mastered the OCF and all her check rides. Now it was time to fly solo. She taxied down the runway, building speed. At 86 knots—nearly a hundred miles an hour—she pulled up the nose of the plane and lifted into the air. It was exhilarating . . . but there was a lot to keep track of. She couldn't fully appreciate the moment until later. When she did, Tammie Jo marveled at the experience, and the path her life had taken to get there. She thought back to her days on her family's farm.

"I felt like a steer who'd broken out of his pen," she mused later. "It was like I'd gotten away with something."

By now Tammie Jo hardly noticed that she was the only woman in her entire squadron—until the solo debrief meeting loomed the next day. Suddenly, being female was going to present a very unique challenge.

Like military bases everywhere, the air station at Corpus Christi was rich in tradition. One particular custom for those who had flown solo for the first time kept Tammie Jo from sleeping the night before. Tradition dictated that after sharing a fun anecdote, the instructor would cut off the student pilot's shirt. Nervous, Tammie Jo wore three T-shirts to the ceremony. Fortunately, her instructor respectfully allowed Tammie Jo to cut off *his* shirt instead.

Initially, future female pilots trained with an abbreviated syllabus. This meant that the requirements for women were different than for men. That rule changed when Tammie Jo was going through flight school. Now, in order to earn navy wings, men and women were expected to qualify with the same criteria, despite the fact that the law still prevented females from flying in combat. So, like everyone in her class, Tammie Jo would learn to land and take off from an aircraft carrier. Before flying onto the flat-decked ship, however, first she practiced on a painted strip of tarmac. Next up was the real thing.

The first time Tammie Jo did a carrier landing and takeoff was with the USS *Lexington*, the famed aircraft carrier that had been the United States' first to include female crewmembers. Now it had been repurposed for use as a training facility for naval aviators. High above, Tammie Jo flew in an oval pattern, waiting her turn to touch down on the carrier. She was flying solo—instructors stayed out of the cockpit for this exercise. Below her, the carrier looked tiny. It was a postage stamp in the middle of endless miles of ocean.

Landing on a Postage Stamp

The USS *Lexington* used a mechanical system to assist the landing and takeoff of planes at sea. Unlike a runway on the ground, an aircraft carrier provides a relatively tiny—and moving—target in the middle of the ocean. Even on a calm day, ocean swells can cause an unstable surface for landing. Then there is the limited runway. Compared to the 2,300 feet (610 meters) of a regular, on-the-ground airstrip, only about 500 feet (150 meters) of the deck of a carrier are available for landing planes. Because of this, each incoming plane is equipped with a giant hook, which, along with the landing gear, is released just before touching down. The hook attaches onto one of four cables strung across the deck of the carrier and catches the plane. Called an arrested landing, there is absolutely no room for error.

Adrenaline pumping, Tammie Jo reminded herself that she'd practiced many times on land—she knew what to do. Aiming her plane at the carrier, she flew in and lowered the landing gear and the hook, which caught one of the arresting cables. There was no time to relax. To add to the challenge, the instructors had planned only a minute between landings; Tammie Jo was just one of several pilots completing the exercise that day. Other pilots would be coming in—and taking off—one after the other.

With the next plane already lining up behind her, Tammie Jo needed to get out of the way *ASAP*. Crewmembers scrambled to set up the catapult assist—the "cat shot." This steam-powered catapult would help hurl her plane back into the sky. When Tammie Jo took off with the assist, she accelerated to 150 mph (240 kph) within three seconds.

The feeling of the launch was powerful! Tammie Jo's body reacted to the jolt of the catapult as it flung her plane out over the ocean. Taking a few extra moments to revel in the joy of the moment, she flew her plane low until easing the nose to a higher altitude.

The next phase, Advanced Jet Training, involved flying the Douglas A-4 Skyhawk, a true fighter jet. Tammie Jo also learned about foreign weapons capabilities and how to evade capture if she ever found herself in enemy territory. She participated in practice exercises including dropping mock bombs and strafing, even though laws still prohibited women from serving in actual combat. There was another critical way for her to contribute, however.

For the next few years, Tammie Jo spent her time as an instructor for novice pilots, including one assignment where she was the flight instructor in charge of the out of control flights. For most people, an OCF instructor was one of the least desired jobs, but Tammie Jo's calm demeanor and excellent ability were real assets for future combat pilots. What she was teaching them could someday save their lives.

Tammie Jo served in the navy until 1995. Transitioning to civilian life, she worked briefly as a pilot hired to fight forest fires. Then she set her sights on Southwest Airlines. Despite it being a fiercely competitive job market, after earning a rating to fly the Boeing 737 commercial airline, Tammie Jo was offered a job. She was one of few women in the field.

The position with Southwest was another dream come true. Soon, though, Tammie Jo was faced with the biggest crisis of her life. After decades of being a pilot, she would need to tap into every technique and nuance she'd ever learned about how to fly a plane. When flight 1380 experienced a catastrophic malfunction, Tammie Jo heroically helped save 148 passengers and crewmembers from certain death.

At first, April 17, 2018, started with the familiar routine. Tammie Jo, now a captain, was flying with Darren Ellisor, her first officer, on the flight scheduled to fly from LaGuardia,

New York, to Dallas, Texas. The travel time was supposed to be 3 hours and 47 minutes. They never made it to Dallas.

WHAM! About 20 minutes into the flight at an altitude of 32,000 feet, the plane jolted violently to the side. *Did another plane just hit us?* Tammie Jo wondered initially. It wasn't another plane but a mechanical failure. Pieces from the engine tore off, damaging the wing and tail of the plane. A section of the debris smashed out one of the windows, and a terrific roaring noise engulfed the plane, still flying at 500 miles an hour. As air bolted from the plane, oxygen masks dropped from the panels above each seat. Along with the air exiting from row 14's broken window, the woman sitting there was partially pulled through the damaged window. Tragically, despite the efforts of other passengers and crew, the woman did not survive.

Meanwhile, in the cockpit, Tammie Jo managed to slow the plane down. Next, she and Darren had to figure out how to land the broken plane so there would be no additional loss of life. It was a daunting task. All the while, Tammie Jo wondered if another piece of the plane, perhaps something even more critical, would fly off as well. She put that out of her mind and concentrated on the task, describing it later as "a little like driving through a boulder field."

Tammie Jo and Darren remained professional, going through safety checks and determining what to do next. Their priority was to find the nearest airport for an emergency landing. They had already descended 18,000 feet (5,500 m) in the first five minutes after the engine failure. Tammie Jo radioed air traffic control to apprise them of the situation. Her voice sounded calm and in control, though she knew that there was no guarantee they would all survive.

After securing a plan for landing, Tammie Jo made her one call into the cabin: "We're not going down . . . We are going to Philly." Next she concentrated on making that promise a reality.

Ultimately, Tammie Jo and Darren were able to land the plane, but there was danger and uncertainty until the last moments. Thankfully, there was no additional loss of life, and when the landing gear finally touched down on the tarmac at Philadelphia's international airport, Tammie Jo unbuckled her seatbelt. She left Darren so she could address the passengers in person.

As Tammie Jo made her way through the cabin reassuring people and answering questions, she was awestruck by their polite gratitude and composure. She had expected chaos, maybe even anger. When airstairs arrived and the passengers could leave, she gave them hugs as they exited. After the cabin emptied, she murmured a prayer of thanks.

Later, Tammie Jo reflected on the loss of the one passenger's life and the near disaster for everyone else. She credited her experience and training for the outcome of the flight. "In the moment, adrenaline will not give you an epiphany beyond what is already within you, what you have already taken time to learn or know."

Tammie Jo's faith, her stubborn determination to become a pilot, and her dogged adherence to intense training and incredible challenges—these are the things that helped Tammie Jo save 148 souls on Southwest flight 1380. She is forever grateful.

Follow Tammie Jo Shults Online

Website: www.captainshults.com

Instagram: @captainshults

Twitter: @captainshults

Facebook: Tammie Jo Shults

Katie Higgins Cook: Blue Angel Icon

It was noisy on the tarmac, but the jet engines behind her didn't drown out Captain Katie Higgins's voice. She stood in front of the open cargo bay of the C-130 Hercules, an airplane that was part of the US Navy and Marine Corps aerial demonstration team known as the Blue Angels. With her crewmembers behind her and today's ride-along passengers in front, Katie went through the preflight briefing. She stood tall, the first female Blue Angels pilot since the team's inception in 1946.

Clasping her hands in front of her, Katie began by introducing the other pilot who would help her fly today, Major Dusty Cook. She was wearing the distinctive uniform of the Blue Angels, a tan garrison cap and a blue flight suit with yellow contrasting. Over her right breast was the insignia for the elite team. On her left arm was a patch of the American flag. Poised and confident, she explained the sequence of maneuvers that the team would soon perform. These, she explained, were similar to maneuvers implemented in combat.

Done with her briefing, she and the others took their places inside the airplane affectionately dubbed "Fat Albert" because of its shape and size. While mostly used as a support aircraft for the Blue Angels team, the C-130 opened each airshow before the fighter jets took to the skies. Now, Katie strapped into the left-hand seat in the cockpit—today she would be the lead pilot for the eight-and-a-half-minute demonstration.

The four turboprop engines were spinning as Katie taxied the nearly 100-foot-long aircraft into position. A crewmember stood above an open port on top of the plane. He held tight to an American flag and waved to the spectators for today's show. As the flag rippled in the breeze, Katie and her crew ran through the last of their safety checks.

Satisfied that all was as it should be, Katie affirmed that they were ready to go. The plane's systems were complex, and the cockpit was filled with switches and equipment, but Katie knew exactly what she was doing. She had to! With complicated maneuvers including low-flying passes and steeply banked turns, there was no leeway for mistakes. She glanced at the small hula girl ornament attached to the dashboard, the traditional good luck charm for the team. Then she initiated the takeoff.

Barreling down the runway, Katie gained enough speed to pop the aircraft off the ground. She retracted the landing gear, and, accelerating to approximately 160 knots (about 184 miles per hour), the plane's nose slanted skyward. Next, she executed the "push over," a leveling off that gave the people inside the plane a moment of weightlessness. If she wasn't firmly cinched into the pilot's seat, Katie would have floated into the air herself for those several seconds.

Settling quickly, it was now time to demonstrate the capability of Fat Albert, something Katie loved to do. She dipped the wings, first right, then left. Swinging down 300 (91 m) feet above the ground, she positioned the plane into a move called a parade pass, banking the plane at 60 degrees. Setting up for the next sequence, she traded altitude for airspeed. She began a controlled descent to 40 feet (12 m) above the ground. Accelerating to 320 knots (370 mph), she demonstrated the sheer size and maneuverability of the C-130. Too soon, after a few more moves, it was time for the landing.

This part was perhaps the trickiest part of the sequence. Katie initiated a sharp descent that, to the inexperienced, looked like the plane was about to crash. She flew the plane slowly, close to stall speed—the rate at which the airplane is no longer generating lift over the wing. The challenge was not to let that happen. Luckily, Katie knew precisely what to do, as she had practiced it hundreds of times. After dropping the landing gear and flaps, the crew went through the final safety checks.

The crowd on the ground hushed as Katie landed Fat Albert on the "deck," applying the maximum braking pressure. Then, with a fun pop up of the plane's nose from the ground, she taxied the plane off the runway. She, along with the rest of the crewmembers, had just flown one of the military's coolest planes.

The Blue Angels

On June 15, 1946, a squad of navy pilots performed in a public exhibition in Jacksonville, Florida. This was the first demonstration of the team that was to become known as the Blue Angels. Now, more than 75 years later, the team's mission has remained the same: "to show-case the teamwork and professionalism of the US Navy and Marine Corps by inspiring a culture of excellence and service to country through flight demonstrations and community outreach." The team first consisted of three planes, five pilots, and 12 support members. Today's Blue Angels include over a hundred people, including pilots and support personnel. Six F/A-18 jets fly in each airshow along with Fat Albert. Despite its playful nickname, this large C-130 cargo plane plays a critical role on the team. In addition to its demonstration performances, Fat Albert flies more than 140,000 miles per season transporting crewmembers, equipment, and spare parts.

Katie's path to becoming a member of the Blue Angels was, in hindsight, maybe not surprising. Both her grandfathers were aviators, and her dad is a retired navy fighter pilot. Katie was born in Jacksonville, Florida, but her family moved around a lot—growing up, she lived in California, Rhode Island, Florida, Virginia, Maryland, and even a couple of years in Japan. Maybe because of the constant changes, or maybe because of her family's legacy, Katie was an adventurous child. Despite her father telling her to "never climb up somewhere you can't get down," she loved to climb to the highest top of trees. She swam competitively, and though she joined the Girl Scouts, she preferred tagging along to her brother's Boy Scouts where she could practice archery and shooting.

When she was around eight years old, Katie attended a Blue Angels airshow. She loved it. After the performance, she stopped at a marine recruitment booth at the show site where a pull-up bar had been set up. Katie did a 30-second flexed arm hang in order to win a marine T-shirt. She wore it proudly. Later, she went home and filled her bedroom walls with posters of airplanes.

As Katie grew up, she mulled over what she wanted to be. Her family had instilled in her the idea of service, and she knew that whatever career she chose, she wanted to contribute to society. Maybe she could be a firefighter. Or a policewoman? She even considered the convent but set that notion aside when she realized she eventually wanted children and a family. Visiting her relatives near the "Space Coast" of Florida each summer, Katie gazed skyward. Sally Ride, the first American woman to fly into space, was one of her heroes.

Whatever path she took, it was evident from early on that Katie was destined for something great. She decided in high school to apply to the US Naval Academy in Annapolis, Maryland. She knew the competition to get in was going to be fierce, so she threw herself into her schoolwork and joined sports and clubs. In 2004, when she graduated from W. T. Woodson High School in Fairfax, Virginia, she was chosen valedictorian of her class. By then, she had already applied—and been accepted—to the US Naval Academy. She was excited, but nervous, too.

Applying to USNA

USNA, the US Naval Academy, trains future naval and marine officers. Each year approximately 3,000 people qualify for acceptance into the academy, but only 1,400 are given appointments—offers to attend. Applying to the academy takes many steps. Applicants must be between 17 and 23 years old and US citizens by the time they begin. They must show strong academics and high scores on standardized tests. Different than regular colleges, USNA requires applicants to secure a nomination from an official source, such as a Congressperson or Senator. The President or Vice President of the United States can also provide this nomination. With these credentials in hand, applicants must pass a medical and fitness test, where they are assessed for coordination, strength, and endurance. Once enrolled, male and female students are called midshipmen. All tuition and room and board expenses are paid for, and midshipmen earn a bachelor's degree when they graduate.

For Katie, high school had been easy. She expected to breeze through the academic part of the program, but classes at the naval academy were surprisingly demanding. She told herself that this was a good thing. Determined and smart, she hunkered down to study and do her best. In 2008, she graduated as a second lieutenant with a bachelor's degree in political science. Because of her outstanding academic record, she was given the opportunity to complete a master's degree. A year later she added a master's degree in international security to her resume. Now it was time to become a marine.

The Marine Basic Course was Katie's next challenge. She headed to Quantico, Virginia, for the six-month training. It was tough! Standards to pass were the same for men and women, so Katie's short stature and 130-pound frame was a huge disadvantage. In order to complete 15-mile hikes wearing a 70-pound pack, she had to take up to four strides for each one stride of the larger men in her platoon. On weekends when others were relaxing and having fun, Katie hit the gym. She knew she couldn't afford any downtime if she were going to pass this course.

Women in the Marines

Rumor has it that during the War of 1812, Lucy Brewer disguised herself as a man so she could serve in the Marine Corps aboard the USS *Constitution*. However, the first *official* female marine was Opha May Johnson who, in 1918, was enlisted for clerical duty along with about 300 other women that same year. Since then there have been many milestones for women in the US Marine Corps. Until recently, certain jobs were off limits to women. It wasn't until December 3, 2015, that Defense Secretary Ashton Carter announced, "There will be no exceptions." He was referring to the law that excluded women from some roles in the military. Starting January 1, 2016, all who qualified, men or women, would be able to serve in any position within the military.

Throughout Katie's time in the marines and throughout her career, she has often felt moments of doubt. *Can I do this? Should I quit?* In the US Naval Academy, she came up against classmates who told her she wasn't going to make it. Later, in flight school after the Basic Course, she failed a couple of flights—mostly due to nerves. She had one chance left. If she messed up one more flight, she would not earn her wings, the certification needed to fly in the military. During this last hurdle, Katie called up her mom. "Will you still be proud of me if I'm not a pilot anymore?" she asked her tentatively.

"Of course." Her mom flew down to support Katie as she flew her next, critical flight. Katie passed it with no problems, proving that she was a competent naval aviator.

Katie credits part of her success to external sources. Sometimes it was to prove others wrong. If someone said she was going to fail, she needed to show them otherwise. She also deeply wanted to make her family proud. Lastly, she knew that as a woman, her accomplishments would make it easier for the other women who would come after her.

Initially, Katie wasn't supposed to deploy to Afghanistan. Another female pilot was listed to go. Then, when that pilot was diagnosed with a medical issue, Katie suddenly found herself heading into hostile territory. She would be flying a more current version of the C-130 Hercules that was used by the Blue Angels. Her pre-deployment workups, the preparation training, was shortened and sped up. For example, when she arrived in country, she had never fired live missiles from an airplane. She soon got that opportunity.

In Afghanistan, Katie's daily routine was mostly the same. She woke up around 5:00 AM and went into the "chow hall" to get her breakfast to go. The friendly Pakistani cooks always had Katie's omelet with mushrooms and a side chunk of pineapple ready to go when she arrived. Next it was time for the daily pre-brief.

Each workday began with Katie and the other crewmembers meeting to learn their mission for the day. They might be hauling cargo or dropping parachutists or leaflets—these warned the local population of an impending battle or were an appeal for information. Since the C-130 could carry large fuel pods on the sides of the plane, sometimes the mission was to provide the fuel for other planes. When these pods were substituted for munitions, Katie's team could also be called in to drop missiles.

Katie knew that she'd joined the marines to serve. But one day when her team got a radio call for help, and she was in the pilot seat, the reality of exactly what that meant became exceedingly clear.

The plane was flying at about 13,000 feet (4,000 m) in a mountainous region of Afghanistan when a voice came over the radio. There had been an insurgent ambush. A group of marines was trapped by enemy forces firing at them from a nearby building. The "TIC" call (troops in contact) indicated the highest level of distress. Over the radio, Katie could hear the machine gun rounds exploding as the marine on the ground called for help.

Katie's training kicked in, and she honed her focus to precisely what she needed to do next. She listened as the marine on the ground conducted a "9-line," the list of instructions Katie and her crew would need to support them.

This is the target.

This is your run-in.

This is where I am . . .

The C-130 could fire Griffin or Hellfire missiles—but they needed to get to the right location. Katie followed the sequence of steps, hyper-focused but with adrenaline kicking in. *This is game time. We have to do this correctly. There is no option to fail.* At the last minute she executed a 360-degree turn to get into the correct position to fire off two missiles.

Immediately there was dead silence.

The next 20 seconds felt like forever. Then the radio came to life. "Okay, we're good."

With the enemy eliminated, Katie and her crewmembers had just saved the lives of these marines. But that wasn't the end of the story. Months later, Katie was at a restaurant in Spain with her fellow crewmembers when someone approached her from behind.

"Hey, were you on Filth 02?" This was the call sign for the C-130 airplane Katie had been flying in Afghanistan. Unbelievably, the marine had recognized Katie's voice since there were so few female pilots at the time. "Yeah," the man told her. "You saved our lives."

Katie would experience one more deployment, though this time it was for another purpose. Now, Katie was stationed in Uganda, on a humanitarian mission. Between her duties, there was time to meet the locals, feed a giraffe, and go to church. It was a different side of the marines, and Katie loved it.

While in Africa, Katie received a call. Would she be interested in flying with the Blue Angels? *Of course!* Several years younger than previous pilots, Katie was surprised—and honored—when she was offered a position.

The time with the Blue Angels was busy. With only one day off per week, Katie dove into the whirlwind of performing, transporting supplies and people, and doing community outreach. The workweek began on Tuesday. Katie came into the Blue Angels headquarters around 8:00 AM, and after quickly checking emails, she attended the day's flight briefing with both the Fat Albert and fighter jet pilots in attendance. Then it was time to fly, though Tuesday was a practice day. Wednesday was more of the same but also included time for the pilots to sign autographs at the National Naval Aviation Museum located near the training base.

On Thursdays Katie and the others packed up Fat Albert and flew to the weekend's next show site. Blue Angel performances for the public were on the weekends. These could be anywhere. Once there, Friday was dedicated to community outreach. Katie might be speaking at a school or hospital. She was also involved in the Make a Wish organization, where she and others would visit sick children to offer support and kindness. Then, there was usually time for more practice before the airshow on Saturday. Sunday was when they packed up and headed back to base. There was a reason why the length of service for pilots on the team was only two to three years. It was a fast-paced life!

Finishing up her time with the Blue Angels, Katie moved into another leadership position. This time she was an airfield operations commander. Under her, 130 marines provided fuel, firefighting, scheduling, and airfield maintenance support. Her marines prepared for the eventuality that American forces might need to build a quick, but temporary airfield out of the country.

This position finished, and Katie made a huge decision. She was not ready to leave the military entirely, but she was married by now—to her former copilot on the Blue Angels— and she wanted to start a family. Moving from active duty to the part-time reserves component of the US military was the best of both worlds. Today, Katie has a civilian job, and she and her husband are raising three beautiful children. As part of her reserves duty, she attends a once-a-month training as well as two weeks of drill every summer. As busy as she is, Katie continues to make time to speak to various groups or conduct interviews.

Despite her fame, Katie remains humble and dedicated to serving others. She has plenty of advice for young people, but one of her personal mottos is: "Calm seas don't make a skilled sailor." She explains, "It's when things go poorly, when you fail at something. It's the hard times that shape you as a person."

Katie is a servicemember's role model. She is also a mom, a pilot, and a business leader. She continues to inspire others to never quit and to take on life's challenges. She knows that these qualities are what make you strong.

Follow Katie Higgins Cook Online

Website: http://katieanncook.com/

Instagram: @gearupflapsup

Twitter: @gearupflapsup

Facebook: Katie Ann Cook

Olga Custodio: Where There's a Will

Querer es poder—Where there's will, there's a way. Olga Custodio played her mantra over and over in her head as she stepped inside the Reserve Officer Training Corps office—the ROTC—after graduating early from high school and enrolling at the University of Puerto Rico. Ever since she'd been a little girl, Olga had wanted to serve her country in the military, specifically in the air force. Here was her chance.

Instead, the captain in charge quickly dismissed Olga and suggested she join a sorority instead.

"No, I want to wear the uniform," Olga insisted.

The officer shrugged and gave her the military entrance exam. Olga answered the questions—and eventually, she would find out that she'd earned one of the highest scores. But that wasn't what the recruiter told her when she went back to the office a couple of weeks later. Instead, he told her, "You didn't pass."

Crushed, Olga set aside her dream of becoming an air force officer. She focused instead on attending college, getting a job, and getting married. What she didn't realize at the time was that it wasn't her test score that had disqualified her but her gender. While the law excluding females from becoming air force officers ended in 1969, not everyone was happy with that change.

Nearly 10 years later a chance encounter reignited Olga's dream. She was at an open house event where there was a booth set up for the air force. A man in a flight suit stood behind the table. When Olga casually walked over and picked up a pamphlet, she learned that the air force was looking for females! *This is my moment!*

By now, Olga was 25 years old, just a few months shy of the age limit for the air force pilot training program. Needing to act fast, she searched for a recruitment office nearby, but all she could find was one for the army. No matter—she would start there. Olga hurried inside.

"What opportunities do you have for a female in army aviation?" she asked. Then she made the mistake of sharing that she was married and that she had a three-and-a-half-year-old daughter.

The recruiter quickly ended the conversation. Olga was not welcome to apply.

Still, Olga wasn't ready to give up. She looked for someone else to process her application before it was too late. But who?

Finally, Olga found a staff sergeant who offered to help, though he had never recruited an officer before.

"No problem," Olga told him; they would work through the steps together.

The sergeant got to the section on the form where Olga needed to designate her top three career choices. What did she want him to fill in?

"Pilot, pilot, and pilot," Olga answered.

Weeks later, the air force contacted Olga. She was in! It was one day before her 26th birthday, the cutoff for acceptance.

Women in the Air Force

When President Truman signed the Women Armed Services Integration Act in 1948, the law stated that females were to have permanent military status, though in clerical or medical positions only. Esther Blake signed up to be the first non-pilot female in the US Air Force. However, it was the navy, not the air force, that graduated the first female aviators in 1974. The army soon followed with female helicopter pilots. The air force opened its pilot training program to women two years later. But there was a catch. By law, women were not allowed to fly in combat situations, and it took until 1993 for that to change. Jeannie Leavitt, now a major general, was at the top of her pilot training class in 1992. When combat restrictions were lifted a year later, Jeannie became the first female fighter jet pilot. She flew over 3,000 flight hours, including 300 in combat. Today, about 21 percent of the US Air Force is female, though women make up less than 6 percent of pilots.

When Olga joined the air force, she fulfilled a lifelong desire to serve her country. She admits that her family background and unique childhood had been highly influential in helping her make that decision. Though she was born in Puerto Rico to two Spanish speakers, Olga spent most of her early years living in different parts of the world. Her father was a sergeant and a military instructor for the army. His job took him all over the world to serve in diplomatic posts. Lucky for the family, he was able to bring them with him.

As a result of her father's career, Olga went to kindergarten and first grade in Taiwan. The family lived on a military base where an old bomb shelter was still set up in their backyard. To Olga, it made a fun playhouse. Next, after a brief stint in New Jersey, Olga, her parents, and her younger brother were stationed in Iran. One vivid memory of her time in the country's capital city, Tehran, was when, each day, vendors would hawk bread, fruits, and vegetables from the backs of donkeys. Olga completed sixth grade before her father's job relocated the family to one last overseas assignment. This time they lived in Paraguay. Though she could already speak fluent Spanish, Olga now learned to read and write the language.

Each time Olga moved, she was immersed in a new culture. Seeing how other people lived opened Olga's eyes, and she developed a deep respect and appreciation for differences. The travel created a powerful sense of resilience in Olga, too. She got used to adapting and to starting over.

When her father retired and the family settled back in Puerto Rico, Olga had enough credits to graduate after her junior year of high school. Suddenly, at 16 years old, Olga needed to figure out what to do next. She felt a deep urge to follow in her father's footsteps, though in the air force instead of the army. When she enrolled at the University of Puerto Rico, she initially chose a major in math, planning to serve in the ROTC program and then the air force. When that didn't work out, she switched to a more practical degree and earned a bachelor's degree in business management.

When Olga was finally accepted into the air force, she began Flight Screening Pilot Officer Training in January 1980. If she passed, the next step was Officer Training School (OTS) where she would earn a commission as a second lieutenant. Then she would go to actual flight school. At last, Olga had the chance to fulfill her dream.

The first two phases of her military training were difficult, but Olga was determined to pass no matter what. She did well, earning a commission as a second lieutenant. The next hurdle was Undergraduate Pilot Training (UPT), the final qualification necessary before becoming an air force pilot. At first, there was one other woman in Olga's class, but she soon dropped out.

For Olga, quitting wasn't an option. "I waited 10 years to start my military career," she told herself. Now that she had this extraordinary opportunity, she threw herself into giving it all she had. If she didn't succeed, it wasn't going to be because she hadn't tried hard enough.

Drinking Water from a Firehose

This phrase describes the furious pace of learning and practicing during Undergraduate Pilot Training (UPT). There are three phases during this one-year program. Before ever getting into a plane, future pilots spend long days studying topics such as aircraft systems, regulations, instruments, navigation, and weather. Provided they pass every test, students go on to phase two, which includes more academics, simulator exercises, and real flight time. Student pilots practice various maneuvers and complete their first solo flight. At the end of this phase, students must choose a track. They'll decide if their focus will be flying heavy transport planes, fighter jets, or helicopters. For phase three of the course, students get in more flying time with a specific aircraft. If all goes well, graduates earn their "wings" (pilot qualifications) at the end of UPT.

UPT was challenging and even exhilarating, though there were also moments that required Olga to face the somber parts as well. "We need to take a footprint impression," the clerk told Olga early in the course. She had already provided her dental records and fingerprints. The footprint was one more grim reminder of the dangers of flying a supersonic jet. If Olga were to crash, the cleanup crew would need a way to identify her remains.

Each day the student pilots were pushed a little more. Emergency training was a top priority. For example, to get used to what it would be like if a pilot had to eject from her plane and parachute to safety, the class practiced a type of modified parasailing behind a truck. With a rope attached between her and the truck, Olga felt her parachute fill and lift as the vehicle accelerated. When she was about 300 feet (91 m) from the ground, the trainer released the tether. Olga floated down— onto a cactus. "I'm done for today," she announced.

"Oh, no. You'll do it again." This time the trainer waited for Olga to get higher, about 500 feet(152 m), before releasing the rope and watching as she landed safely, luckily into empty desert.

Another part of the course involved recognizing the symptoms of oxygen deprivation. For this aspect of the training, students rode in a plane carrying an altitude chamber. At about 38,000 feet (11,600 m), trainers at first simulated a slow depressurization. Olga was given a writing pad to record the sensations she was feeling. How did the loss of oxygen feel? What telltale signs did she notice while it was happening? She was given math equations to solve and other cognitive exercises. The next drill involved a rapid depressurization of the chamber. Olga found that she had about a minute of useful consciousness. If this ever happened in real life, those few seconds of rational thought would mean the difference between life and death.

Olga moved on to the next portion of the training. A special, custom helmet was made for her, molded to fit her head perfectly. She started in a T-37 airplane, a training jet where the pilot and student sat side by side. Next would be the T-38 Talon, the supersonic aircraft that was one step away from the fighter jets used in combat. Here, the student pilot sat in front, and an instructor sat directly behind. Olga soon had a chance to practice flying solo.

It was during one of her very first solo flights that Olga experienced an emergency that could have ended her career—or worse. She had just taken off when a turkey buzzard, an enormous bird with a wingspan of up to five feet, crashed into her windshield. The glass stayed intact, thankfully, but visibility was now significantly impaired. How on Earth was Olga going to land when she could barely see? Her training kicked in, and she played back the emergency protocol: *aviate, navigate, communicate*. She analyzed the situation. Her engine was still functioning, and, as far as she could tell, nothing was broken or cracked. She quickly communicated her situation. Soon, another airplane deployed to do a visual of her aircraft, confirming that the plane didn't appear to be damaged. Olga was cleared to land. Now she had to figure out how.

With emergency vehicles lined up on the tarmac, Olga lowered the plane, relying heavily on instrument navigation since there was no way to see past the windshield. It wasn't until she was safely on the ground that the magnitude of the situation hit her. It would have been so easy to have gotten disoriented and crashed the plane. The fact that she had not only survived but remained calm and focused during the emergency validated her purpose. She really *was* meant to be a pilot. Others thought so, too.

As Olga mastered the complex requirements of flying a supersonic jet, her instructors were mostly encouraging. Then, one day a guest instructor came to fly with the student pilots. The purpose of having guest instructors was to bring a different perspective to each potential fighter pilot. Theirs were another set of expert eyes to make sure that absolutely nothing was being overlooked or left to chance. When Olga met with this new instructor, she was unpleasantly surprised by his negativity.

"Why are you here?" the man asked her bluntly. "You're not going to make it through this program."

Instead of letting the man's comments discourage her, Olga reminded herself of her motto: *querer es poder.* She did have the will, and now she'd been given the way. *I'll show him I can do it*, Olga told herself. She pushed herself harder, her new-found energy and grit propelling her to graduate in the top 5 percent of her class.

When Olga completed flight school, she became the first Latina military pilot in the US Air Force. While regulations had not caught up to her yet—women were still excluded from flying in combat at the time—Olga could still serve her country in a valuable way. She earned her Fighter-Attack-Reconnaissance rating, the qualification needed to fly as an instructor pilot in the supersonic T-38 jet trainer. Now she could help others become expert jet pilots, too.

"Are you sure?" At first, Olga's male students questioned her constantly whenever she gave them a command. She didn't let their doubts get to her. Instead, she pulled out the training manual and backed up her instructions with facts from the book. Her patience paid off. As Olga's students graduated, they thanked her over and over. She earned a reputation of excellence and was soon assigned to the most challenging students. Her teaching methods paid off, and she helped many students become superb pilots.

In 1988, Olga wanted to spend more time with her family, which now included two young children, and decided to make a career change. She shifted from active military status to the reserves. While she would still be in the military, it would no longer be her full-time career. She applied to be a commercial airline pilot.

Olga made history again with American Airlines when she was hired as the first Latina pilot in the company's history and later rose to the position of captain. As Olga shifted her focus to commercial flying, she reflected on what she had enjoyed about flying for the military. Flying a military jet included acrobatics such as loops, cloverleafs, and formation flying, in which multiple planes could be as close as three feet back and three feet apart from each other. In her fighter jet, she felt the speed and sense of power.

But commercial flying had its joys as well. For each flight she was no longer alone or flying with just one other student. Now there was a whole team, not only in the flight deck, but also in the back of the plane with the passengers and crewmembers. It was fun and exhilarating to collaborate and to be in charge. One flight in particular summed up Olga's feeling of gratitude for the direction her life had taken.

The flight that day was to Washington, DC. By then, Olga had been flying internationally as well as all over the United States. It wasn't her first time into DC. As she flew above the Potomac River on her approach to the airport, she communicated with the tower that she was ready to land. However, there was another airplane in her space on the runway. She would need to delay her approach.

The sun was setting as Olga circled over the city. Dusk descended, and the lights in the nation's capital flickered on. Olga flew by the National Mall, taking in the monuments and the awe-inspiring beauty of the scene below. Here she was over the nation's capital, serving her country as an airline captain and a US Air Force Reserve officer. It was a powerful moment.

Today, though Olga is retired, she is as busy as ever. She is passionate about speaking to young people, especially to encourage them to apply to science, technology, engineering, and math (STEM) fields, and to contribute to the country and to the world. Every time she speaks, she reminds her audience—and herself—*querer es poder*. Olga had always had the desire. Through grit, hard work, and perseverance, she found the way.

Follow Olga Custodio Online

Website: www.purflygirl.com

Instagram: @olgacustodio

Twitter: @purflygirl

Facebook: Olga E. Custodio

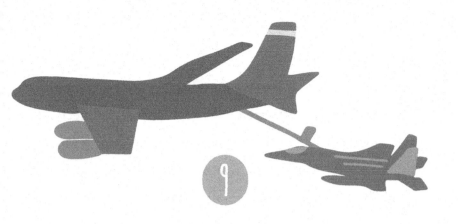

Kimberly Scott Ford: The Glide-Path Forward

The day started early. Kimberly Scott Ford was at the preflight briefing for today's mission on the KC-135 Stratotanker, a hefty plane capable of providing air-to-air refueling for US and allied aircraft. There was a lot to go over, so the initial part of the meeting would last a good two hours. First Kimberly needed to know where she and the two other crewmembers were going—and how to get there. The plane was carrying thousands of pounds of fuel, and it was their job to deliver that fuel on time. Kimberly made sure she understood the exact coordinates of the rendezvous. Get it wrong and any planes that were low on fuel would be forced to abort their missions.

Not on my watch, she vowed.

Today's preflight briefing also included a detailed analysis of the weather, both here at the base and en route to the meet-up location. It was hard enough for the boom operator—the person in charge of the fuel line—to connect the refueling boom to another airplane during calm weather. If high winds or excessive weather was predicted, the task would be almost impossible—and dangerous.

Once Kimberly and the others had gone over the details of the mission, including emergency procedures, they headed to the plane. Using a series of detailed checklists, Kimberly helped to conduct a preflight inspection of the plane itself along with the systems onboard. Although constantly upgraded and modified, the Stratotanker was decades old. It was critical to make sure that everything was working properly, not only for herself and the crew, but also for the planes that were relying on them today. Finally, it was time to close the emergency exit. Kimberly strapped herself into the pilot seat in the cockpit.

Fired up, four turbofan engines propelled the gray-bodied aircraft down the runway. Kimberly eased the heavy plane into the air, accelerating to 500 miles per hour (800 km/h). Now it was up to her and her copilot to get to the refueling location exactly on time. Confident and more than capable, she marveled at the opportunity she had to pilot this plane. It made no difference that she was Black or that she was a woman. Up here in the skies, Kimberly was home.

The Stratotanker

This aircraft, designed by Boeing, was a game changer in aeronautics when the first of its kind took to the skies in 1956. The KC-135 Stratotanker has a primary mission of providing in-flight refueling to other aircraft, though it can also transport cargo or dozens of passengers. There are generally three crewmembers on the Stratotanker: a pilot, copilot, and boom operator. Sometimes there is also a navigator. The boom operator works from the back of the plane where a "flying boom" is used to off-load fuel into various aircraft. This telescoping fuel line extends up to 20 (6 m) feet and connects to a port in the receiving plane, thus solving a huge logistical issue. Because the Stratotanker is able to provide air-to-air refueling, other planes have the flexibility to continue a mission rather than having to return to base when their fuel runs low. Further capabilities for the Stratotanker include a top speed of 530 mph (853 kmph), a range of 1,500 miles (2,400 km), and ample cargo space. Today, the Stratotanker is being phased out by the KC-46 Pegasus, another mid-air refueler.

Kimberly grew up in Bellevue, Washington, a picturesque part of the state with access to plenty of outdoor parks and recreation. Each summer she participated in camps, sometimes to do various service projects. One summer she enrolled in the Young Conservation Corps. There she worked to rehabilitate the trails and help install extra plumbing. It was a chance to give back, and it instilled in Kimberly a keen sense of accomplishment. She determined that she would do something worthy with her life—she just wasn't sure what.

One day Kimberly's parents took her to see the Blue Angels perform. The elite US Navy team often put on airshows to showcase the capability and prestige of their supersonic jets, and today was no different. Except it *was* different for Kimberly. As she savored deep breaths of air laced with the faint smell of jet fuel, something clicked. She watched, intoxicated, as the pilots maneuvered the sleek blue and yellow jets into intricate patterns in the sky. The speed and obvious power of the jets enthralled her. *Could I ever do that?* she wondered.

After the air demonstration, young Kimberly watched as each of the pilots came to greet the crowd. When she saw that they were all men, her elation waned. When Kimberly was a child, the world had unwritten rules about what was acceptable for men and women. Though she was smart and hardworking, being a pilot seemed like an impossible dream. "Young men do that," some of her teachers told her. *Certainly not women* was their obvious message. They tried to steer Kimberly into a more realistic career choice.

The Blue Angels experience was not the first time Kimberly had been spellbound while watching airplanes. Her family had traveled back and forth to Baltimore, Maryland, to visit relatives. From the confines of the airport, Kimberly had watched airliners speed down the runway and lift into the sky. She had even begged her parents to combine her Christmas and birthday gifts so she could travel by herself to Baltimore. For a little girl who was often too shy to talk to strangers, Kimberly had plenty of courage. And drive. She just never thought that *she* would have the chance to be a pilot.

In Kimberly's personal life, her parents presented her with plenty of opportunities and experiences. They took her to museums and lectures, always encouraging her to try new things. She also hiked and swam and went kayaking in the lakes and rivers near her home. She loved the outdoors, and her parents fostered this enjoyment.

Kimberly loved to read, too. She escaped into other worlds with The Chronicles of Narnia and The Lord of the Rings. She pored through books like *Ramona* by Beverly Cleary. Though Kimberly didn't like to speak too much herself, she admired Ramona's adventurous spirit. Her mother steered her toward books about African history, too, and discouraged her from limiting herself to books where girls had only traditional roles. Kimberly read so much that her mother thought she might end up a librarian.

As much as she enjoyed reading, Kimberly had ideas for her life other than being a librarian. At first, she wasn't sure what they were. Could she be some sort of ambassador, which would allow her to travel and see the world? Maybe she could go to Paris and be a model—her father had served as a signal corps officer in France before she was born, and he had loved it. One day she made a comment about how the Black actress who played Lieutenant Uhura on the TV show *Star Trek* was an officer. Her mother responded, "Why not you?"

On the Wings of Others

Throughout US history, there have been more male pilots than female. Even today, the Federal Aviation Administration (FAA) reports that less than 10 percent of today's commercial pilots are women. But ever since the dawn of aviation, women, along with men, have been fascinated by flying high. In the early part of the twentieth century, Bessie Coleman was denied admission to pilot school in the United States because she was of African American and Native American descent. She didn't let that stop her. Bessie traveled to France and earned her international pilot's license in 1921—after learning French. Long-distance pilot Amelia Earhart is another household name. In 1929 she created opportunities for female aviators when she helped establish the first National Women's Air Derby. She later worked to establish the Ninety-Nines, an

> international organization for female pilots, named for
> the number of women who initially joined. A great propo-
> nent of women's rights, Amelia once said, "Women must
> try to do things as men have tried. When they fail, their
> failure must be but a challenge to others."

When Kimberly was in high school, she made a life-changing decision. Influenced by her father's experience, she decided to join the military herself. It had taken real courage for her father to leave his home and family to embark on something so unexpected. But Kimberly loved the idea of contributing to the world and offering her service to others. She first applied to the Reserve Officer Training Corps—ROTC—at the University of Washington. The response was curt and definitive. "These slots are filled. You're not the type of person we're looking for."

Well, what about the Air Force Academy? Kimberly thought, not ready to give up. For the time, it was an unusual choice for a female, and, to top it off, the academy enrolled very few people of color. Despite that, the idea seemed like a good one. For one, the academy would pay for her entire education. If she could stick to it, she could train to be a pilot there. Maybe someday she would work for Alaska Airlines, the commercial airline company based in her hometown. Kimberly filled out all the paperwork for the Air Force Academy, and to her surprise and delight, she was accepted. After she graduated from high school, she headed to Colorado Springs, Colorado, where the academy was located north of the city.

The next four years were demanding. Though Kimberly had earned a high grade point average in high school, her classes there hadn't been that challenging. Here at the academy, Kimberly had to buckle down to work. There were physical obstacles as well. The cadets had to complete a minimum number of push-ups and sit-ups as well as run a mile and a half in a certain amount of time. Since Kimberly was already fit, the push-ups and sit-ups were no problem—she completed the maximum—but running was another story. She had always been a slow runner and had to push herself to pass this portion of the test. Despite the difficulties, initially Kimberly did well. It wasn't until her sophomore year that she felt like quitting.

Kimberly's grades had dipped dangerously low. She'd been spending more time socializing rather than focusing on her schoolwork. Finally, she came to a crossroads. If she wanted to continue, she was going to have to make some drastic changes. But it wasn't just in her academic classes that she'd fallen behind. She was also struggling in the soaring course, the initial step in a series of flight-focused classes. The course was the first opportunity for cadets to experience flying. They practiced in gliders, called sailplanes, and learned the basics of aeronautics. It was a stepping-stone to engine-powered planes.

Kimberly thought long and hard about giving up. She knew she was smart. She'd already been accepted to Stanford

University. Should she leave the air force and go there instead? The temptation to transfer tugged at her. *I don't have to deal with this,* she told herself. Yet . . . did she really want to give up? *No,* she told herself. *I made it this far; I'm going to keep going.*

After passing the soaring course, Kimberly's next phase of flying at the academy was in a Cessna, a small plane with a turboprop engine in front. She ran into another roadblock. This time, though she had resolved to focus on her work, her original instructor wasn't interested in teaching her. Kimberly was African American and a woman, and he thought teaching her would be a waste of time. According to him, she wasn't going to pass anyway, so why bother? Kimberly asked for a reassignment. With a new instructor, she concentrated on passing, and, this time, she did so easily.

Today's Women in Aviation

Peek into the cockpit of any major airline today, and you're still more likely to see men than women sitting at the controls. According to the Federal Aviation Administration (FAA), in 2020 approximately 7 percent of commercial pilots were women. The question is why. Perhaps the biggest reason why there are so few women pilots is that there aren't as many role models. Fortunately, that statistic is changing. Organizations such as Women in Aviation International and the Ninety-Nines help to bring recognition to women interested in this field. And with many commercial airline companies predicting pilot shortages in the years to come, female recruitment is imperative.

Having recommitted herself to graduating from the Air Force Academy, Kimberly sought out extra instruction. She asked for—and received—additional help from her classmates and instructors. She found mentors and like-minded people to encourage her. Though her parents never pushed her, Kimberly also looked to them for the strength she needed to keep going. Step by step she pulled her grades up.

Along with four other women in her class, Kimberly graduated in the spring of 1990. Armed with a bachelor's degree in political science, Kimberly headed to Del Rio, Texas, for a one-year program to learn to be a pilot. In the whole history of the Air Force Academy, she would be only the fourth African American female graduate to take this next step. No matter what, Kimberly resolved to make it.

Compared to her classmates, Kimberly had less experience. Many of them had been flying privately for years. It was a struggle to keep up with the high-level expectations. There was absolutely no margin for error, and doing a simply average job was not good enough.

Luckily, Kimberly found an instructor who became her mentor. Kevin Mastin would later go on to fly in the air force Thunderbirds, an elite demonstration team similar to the Blue

Angels. Still somewhat shy and hesitant to speak out when things weren't going right, Kimberly learned to think fast and to push herself. Kevin had the same attitude. He told her, "You can't accept not performing well." He held her accountable, but also assured her, "You're going to make it through this program. You're going to work hard."

Kimberly did work harder than she ever had, and it paid off. A year later, she earned her "wings." She was now qualified to fly!

Kimberly stayed in active duty status with the air force for over 10 years. After a non-flying job at Fairchild Air Force Base in Washington, she was called to her first assignment as a pilot. She reported to Castle Air Force Base, a strategic air command station in California that has since closed. She would be flying the Stratotanker.

The next several years took her all over the world. She flew in Saudi Arabia, England, Japan, the Middle East, and all over eastern Europe. Her assignments were as varied as the locations. In addition to air-to-air refueling efforts, sometimes she flew humanitarian missions to drop off people and supplies or transport injured servicemembers. Other times she was in charge of flying distinguished visitors—congressmen and VIPs. She flew over 1,000 combat hours, including into Iraq and Afghanistan. Sometimes she landed in dirt fields or at staging areas outside war zones.

Kimberly loved her job and especially the longer flights because that meant she got to stay somewhere new. Every time she packed her duffel bag for a mission, she knew she was doing something important. Finally, in 2001, Kimberly transitioned from active duty to a reserves duty status, serving part-time at McChord Air Force Base in Washington state until January 1, 2016.

Simultaneously, Kimberly decided to apply to be a pilot in the civilian world. She'd always wanted to fly for Alaska Airlines, so when she was offered a position with the company, she didn't hesitate to accept it.

Transitioning to a commercial airliner required several more months of training. But Kimberly was by now an expert pilot—she knew what she was doing. When she completed the course, she was assigned the position of first officer for the Boeing 737 passenger plane. She was Alaska Airlines' first African American female pilot.

Today, life is still busy. When she's scheduled to fly, Kimberly's days start as early as 2:00 AM. She reports to the airport by 5:00 where she does the preflight briefing. There are always two pilots onboard whenever she flies. Sometimes the flight is shorter, such as to Dallas, Texas, and back. When flying longer distances, Kimberly stays overnight at the destination city before flying back to Seattle. Her average schedule involves about 75 to 80 hours of flight time per month.

Working for Alaska Airlines is Kimberly's dream job. She loves the company for its people and for its policy to hire people from a wide variety of backgrounds. Though women, especially minorities, still make up a small fraction of all pilots, Kimberly is helping to change that statistic. She volunteers at events and for organizations such as the Organization of Black Aerospace Professionals, Tuskegee Airman International, and Women in Aviation. She mentors young people, always encouraging them to pursue the things that interest them most. Kimberly believes in "giving forward." She has important advice for all her mentees. "It's okay to fail. Maintain a positive attitude. Be prepared and persistent."

She thinks back to all her own mentors, to the veterans who coached her over the years, and especially the Tuskegee Airmen. She says, "No matter who you are, you're going to face a challenge. Whatever you do, you must give it a shot."

Humble, grateful, passionate, Kimberly works with others to help them find their own glide path forward.

Follow Kimberly Scott Ford Online

Website: http://baap.info/?p=1191

Twitter: @Kimberlysford68

10

Ronaqua Russell:
Semper Paratus—Always Ready

"This is a special place," Coast Guard Admiral Charles Ray said to the crowd gathered for today's ceremony. "This is hallowed ground we're on. These are hallowed skies above us." He looked over the group, pausing to let his words sink in. It was February 21, 2019, and today's participants were gathered at the historic Tuskegee Moton Field, home of the first African American military pilots in US history.

Ronaqua Russell, a Coast Guard pilot, stood motionless, her back straight and her eyes focused ahead. At first she tried to keep her face blank, though a thrill of excitement coursed through her as she listened to the commander's words. The whole ceremony felt surreal. She knew she was the first African American female to receive the prestigious Air Medal, but it was still hard to grasp the enormity of the event. Being at Tuskegee helped make it a little more real, though, because Ronaqua had a personal connection to the location. Her great uncle, First Lieutenant Henry E. Rohlsen, had served as a Tuskegee airman in World War II.

The admiral spoke again. "This is a special place in our nation's history, and today is a special day in our service's history. . . . What she has done is the same thing those Tuskegee Airmen did." He was referring to her courage, the grit and determination she had displayed when battling the savage winds and rain of Hurricane Harvey. Indeed, Ronaqua had risked her life when she and Lieutenant Commander Steve Pittman took off in the first aircraft during the record-breaking weather event.

The citation on Ronaqua's Air Medal award stated, "Due to widespread outages to air traffic control infrastructure, she provided expert navigation through embedded thunderstorms, heavy turbulence, and moderate icing just hours after Hurricane Harvey made landfall."

Ronaqua thought back to her efforts during the days of the hurricane. She knew it was an incredible honor to receive the award, but she couldn't help thinking it was also just part of her job. The Coast Guard didn't only operate when the weather was nice. *Semper Paratus.* The Coast Guard's motto meant "Always ready." Serving when needed, even in bad weather, was just part of why Ronaqua had signed up in the first place. As the admiral pinned on Ronaqua's medal, she couldn't stop grinning.

From Earliest Times ... Women in the US Coast Guard

The origins of today's US Coast Guard begin with the lighthouse. In 1789, Congress determined that it would support and pay for America's 12 light stations, initiating the precursor to the Coast Guard. In addition to maintaining these lifesaving beacons, women such as Ida Lewis and Kate Walker performed dozens of heroic sea rescues. As time passed, the Coast Guard expanded into other areas—as did women's participation. During World War I, women served in clerical roles as uniformed "yeomanettes." During World War II, Congress approved a women's corps, the SPARs (*Semper Paratus*-Always Ready). In 1973, the Coast Guard was the first US military service to open its Officer Candidate School to women. Today, about 15 percent of the 40,000 active-duty Coast Guard servicemembers are women.

Ronaqua grew up on St. Thomas, one of the US Virgin Islands in the Caribbean. Though she lived mostly with her mother and grandparents, she had a large, extended family. Her father lived on the nearby island of St. Croix, and when Ronaqua went to visit him, the option was to go by boat or, frequently, by small commuter airplane. For a while, her mother was in college on the US mainland, and Ronaqua took a plane to visit there, too. She loved the feeling of flying, whether it was the small seaplane to travel from one island to another or a larger commercial plane.

One day her uncle asked her, "What do you want to be when you grow up?"

Ronaqua thought about the flight attendants on the planes she'd flown in. That would be a great way to travel, she thought. Her uncle had a different idea. "I think you should be a pilot." The idea resonated, though it was several years before Ronaqua acted on it.

Ronaqua did well in school, skipping both kindergarten and fourth grade. Perhaps her success wasn't surprising with two high-performing parents who also modelled fierce drive and independence. Her father was a senator in the Virgin Islands government and her mother, Aquannette Chinnery, was a practicing attorney who later worked as an assistant attorney general. In Ronaqua's family it was never an option to slack off. Her grandfather often reminded her about the five P's: Proper planning prevents poor performance.

The family was close-knit and supportive. It seemed there were always others around to offer advice and encouragement. One thing Ronaqua especially enjoyed was singing. Her mother was a beautiful singer who frequently sang in church or at outside events. With her grandmother as her manager, Ronaqua also sang professionally at various venues. One day her singing helped set her life's path in motion.

A couple of pilots from the US Coast Guard were coming to St. Thomas to get married. They'd heard about Ronaqua's singing and booked her to sing at their wedding. At the reception, the newly married pilots started chatting with Ronaqua. What did she plan to do once she finished high school?

"Maybe I'll be a pilot," Ronaqua answered. Thinking of an aunt who was in the navy, she amended her answer, "A navy pilot."

"Have you considered the Coast Guard?" the groom asked her.

Ronaqua hadn't. Did the Coast Guard even have airplanes? Wasn't it just mostly boats? The new bride and groom were eager to explain. While smaller than the other military branches, the Coast Guard had a whole aviation section. Plus, there was a higher chance of getting into flight school through the Coast Guard versus through the air force or army. As Ronaqua listened, the idea took root.

In the summer before her senior year, Ronaqua enrolled in the Coast Guard's Academy Introduction Mission (AIM)—a one-week program designed to introduce high school students to life in the Coast Guard. From entering a robotics competition where teams had to build a boat capable of performing various missions to discovering what life was like the military, it was a busy week. Ronaqua loved it. Then the organizers discovered her musical talent, and they asked her to sing the national anthem at the closing ceremony.

"We would love to have you in the Coast Guard," the director of admissions told Ronaqua. Her path was set—until there was a problem.

Ronaqua would be 16 when she graduated from high school, too young to enter the Coast Guard. To her, the idea of waiting for a year until she was 17 was not an option. Instead, she applied—and got into—an early admissions program at the University of the Virgin Islands (UVI). She would combine her senior year with the first year of college, taking UVI classes in applied mathematics while participating in all the main events at her high school. She had earned a scholarship, too, which she planned to use when she transferred to Columbia University in New York City.

After two years at UVI, Ronaqua ran into another setback. Her scholarship didn't cover tuition for a mainland college. The cost of attending Columbia without it would be staggering. She could take out loans, sure, but it would take years, maybe even a decade, to pay them off. Ronaqua was devastated. She had no backup plan.

"Well, what about the Coast Guard?" her grandmother reminded her.

Ronaqua thought back to the newlywed Coast Guard pilots. *Yes, that is what I will do.* Old enough now, she applied to the Coast Guard Academy—and was soon accepted. Ronaqua was thrilled but also nervous about leaving home. Indeed, it would be a huge culture shock to leave the Virgin Islands, and it would be hard for her to adjust to the military. She decided to join a preparation program first.

When Ronaqua finally entered the Coast Guard Academy, she had a singular focus. She knew she wanted to become an aviator, so she did everything she could to achieve that goal. She joined the Aviation Club and took a newly offered aviation class. *Aviation or bust!* she told herself. During her senior year at the academy, Ronaqua applied to go to flight school next, though 75 others also applied. She was one of 24 who got in.

The Coast Guard doesn't have its own flight school, so future aviators train through the Naval Flight School in Pensacola, Florida. The program has strict rules. Students have only two chances to pass certain tests. If they fail, they are removed from flight school. When Ronaqua failed a check ride—an evaluation flight—early in her training, she knew she had absolutely no room for a less-than-excellent performance going forward. Since every flight could be her last, she made sure she was always as prepared as possible.

Ronaqua pinned her "wings" in 2014—graduating from flight school, she earned the right to wear an aviator's pin on her uniform, thus designating her as a qualified military pilot. The next step would be to train with one of the Coast Guard's specific airplanes. As Ronaqua ranked her aircraft preferences, she hoped to get the C-130 Hercules.

Ronaqua attributes her success to many mentors. One was Jeanine McIntosh-Menze, the first Black female to become an aviator in the Coast Guard and specifically as a pilot for the Hercules. But when Ronaqua received her assignment, it was to fly the HC-144 Ocean Sentry instead. Initially disappointed, Ronaqua reminded herself of something the captain in charge of the Coast Guard cadets had said. Whether a cadet was assigned a fixed wing (airplane) or helicopter, one was still going to fly. "It's like picking your favorite flavor of ice cream," he'd said. "Even if you don't get your first choice, you still get ice cream."

Ronaqua nodded. *Either way, I'm still a pilot.*

The Fab 5

The Coast Guard's "Fab 5" refers to its first group of female African American pilots. These five include Ronaqua Russell, Jeanine McIntosh-Menze, La'Shanda Holmes, Chanel Lee, and Angel Hughes. Each of the women has the designation of being first in something. In addition to being the first African American woman to earn an Air Medal, Ronaqua was the first Black woman to become a Safety Officer. Before her, Jeanine earned her aviator wings in 2005 from the Naval Air Station at Corpus Christi, becoming the first African American female Coast Guard pilot. La'Shanda was the first Black woman to fly a USCG helicopter. When Chanel graduated from the Coast Guard Academy, she made history when she was selected for flight school. In an effort to encourage more women, especially women of color, to become pilots, Angel cofounded an organization called Sisters of the Skies. Today, these five women serve as role models and mentors to others who are interested in flying.

An hour before her graduation ceremony, Ronaqua got a phone call. There was a sudden opening for the HC-144 training. The person slated for the spot had a last-minute medical issue and could no longer attend, so could Ronaqua take his place? Oh, and she would have to start on Monday.

Ronaqua talked to her family. Several of her relatives, many of whom had traveled long distances, were there for her graduation. She wanted to accept the open HC-144 slot, and it was the smart thing to do—it could take months before there was another opening. But her relatives had expected to take the next week to sightsee and enjoy each other's company. Ronaqua thought she'd have a break, too, after the intense past two years of flight school.

"You've got to do it," her mom advised her. "Whenever you get an opportunity, you must take it."

After the winging ceremony, Ronaqua found the man whose place she was taking. They met in the parking lot where he handed her his helmet and a study book. He wished her luck. Now, instead of going on vacation, she and her mom would drive to Alabama. They had two days to get there.

The Ocean Sentry

The USCG Aviation Training Center qualifies students for one of five aircraft: the Jayhawk or Dolphin helicopters or one of three airplanes. The HC-144 Ocean Sentry is a medium range aircraft used mostly for search and rescue, homeland security, and environmental protection and response. It has the endurance to be in the air for over 10 hours, and with sophisticated sensors and avionics, it is perfect for patrolling large search areas. The plane also has a high-tech onboard communication system for relaying secure and nonsecure voice and data messages. Because of this, it can be used as a command platform to coordinate the logistics of an operation. A rear ramp allows the plane to be reconfigured to hold passengers or to serve as a medevac vehicle. This ramp also allows for aerial delivery of equipment and supplies.

After the 12-week program at the USCG aviation center, Ronaqua was qualified to fly the HC-144 Ocean Sentry as a copilot. The next step was to advance to first pilot status and eventually to an aircraft commander. Meanwhile, she headed back to her home unit in Corpus Christi. Now, in addition to flying, she was tasked with various other jobs such as scheduler, safety officer, and property officer in charge of inventory. Soon she would have a chance to serve in a life-or-death crisis, demonstrating exactly what her purpose was in the Coast Guard.

At first, reports came in that there was a tropical disturbance, the precursor to Hurricane Harvey. Ronaqua didn't think too much of it initially. By now a first pilot, she was busy focusing on an annual check ride to assess her proficiency. She was flying with an instructor who would evaluate her skills—success on the test was critical because it enabled her to keep flying.

The check ride went smoothly, and Ronaqua passed with no issues. But now, meteorologists were warning that Hurricane Harvey was going to be a significant and dangerous storm. Though still located in the ocean, it had developed into a category four hurricane. This meant that winds would gust at 130 to 156 miles per hour, and that "catastrophic damage" was certain to occur once it made landfall. The storm, coming later that evening, was going to be bad.

Ronaqua and the other crewmembers hurried into action. Ronaqua's job was to fly supplies and personnel to various staging areas as well as to warn people to evacuate. Her crew flew along beaches, and, whenever they saw someone who hadn't evacuated, they took the plane low and dropped a message block, a written communication to warn of the impending danger.

This is the Coast Guard. Evacuate immediately.

When the storm hit, Ronaqua was ready. Undeterred by driving rain, wind, and often almost no visibility, she and

Commander Steve Pittman were the pilots on the first plane in a sky that was unnervingly empty of other aircraft. They continued to fly through the outer bands of the hurricane, delivering lifesaving supplies and personnel. Using the plane's communication equipment, they helped coordinate rescue efforts when ground systems were no longer functioning. Thousands of people were stranded and needed help. Fast.

Ronaqua joined more than 2,060 Coast Guard servicemembers who worked day and night. She landed on partially flooded runways knowing that her mission was critical. Resting little, a week and a half later Ronaqua was still leading rescue efforts, working at the incident command post, this time from the ground. Hurricane Harvey was spent, but Ronaqua soon received more disturbing news. Another hurricane was forming in the Atlantic, and this one was going to get personal. Hurricane Irma would soon hit the Virgin Islands where Ronaqua's family was living. Unable to evacuate in time, they were forced to shelter in their home.

It was a tense time for Ronaqua. She couldn't help her family and could only pray that they would all be okay. Finally, after dozens of attempts, Ronaqua got through by phone and for one heart-stopping moment she heard her mom's voice—until the call dropped. Another 36 hours passed before she could verify that, while the house was damaged, her mother and other family members were okay. Ronaqua quickly helped to relocate them before a third hurricane hit two weeks later.

This time, Hurricane Maria devastated parts of the Caribbean and especially Puerto Rico. Ronaqua took to the skies, again delivering critical aid.

The size and destruction of the three storms was almost unimaginable. Ronaqua heard somewhere that they'd caused a staggering $188 billion in property damage. Worse, thousands of deaths were attributed to the crisis. Exhausted, but knowing she'd done her part, Ronaqua reflected on her decision to join the Coast Guard. She knew, without a doubt, that she was exactly where she needed to be.

Today, Ronaqua is a Safety Officer at Air Station Miami, in charge of the safe and effective management of the post. When she flies, which is one to three days a week, she supports a variety of missions. These include search and rescue operations, medical evacuations, or law enforcement operations, including the prevention of drug and human trafficking. Her job is extremely varied, and every day brings with it different challenges and responsibilities.

Whatever the day holds, Ronaqua is ready. *Semper Paratus.*

Follow Ronaqua Russell and the US Coast Guard Online

Website: https://www.uscga.edu/2019-inductees/

Instagram: @USCG

Twitter: @USCG

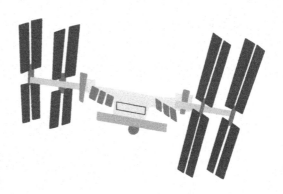

Part III
Outside Earth

(62+ Miles)

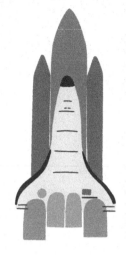

11

Mae Jemison: No Limits

"Houston, Tranquility Base here. The Eagle has landed."

Astronaut Neil Armstrong's voice was steady, though the transmission from the moon was full of static. The response from the Mission Operations Control Room in Houston, Texas, was less composed. "Tranquility, we copy you. You got a bunch of guys about to turn blue. We're breathing again. Thanks a lot."

The broadcast of the first moon landing was on live television. The date was July 20, 1969. Around the world, an estimated 530 million people had tuned in to the live feed, including young Mae Jemison, a 12-year-old girl from Chicago. Already fascinated by space, Mae stared at the incredible feat of ingenuity and precise science and imagined herself doing the same kind of thing when she grew up. But watching the screen from her living room, neither she nor the other viewers outside Mission Control realized how close to failure the astronauts had actually come.

While approximately 400,000 people had helped to make the moon landing a success, there were a million things that could—and almost did—go wrong. For example, Mae didn't know that when the astronauts landed the lunar module, there were less than 30 seconds left of fuel. The astronauts had only one chance to get the mission right. Next, as the module was descending, the computer systems were sending out alert after alert. The astronauts inside admitted afterward that it had been a tense and uncertain few moments. But on that Sunday in July, it seemed to young Mae that with hard work and science, there was nothing people couldn't accomplish.

A few hours later, the next part of the mission unfolded. This time Neil Armstrong, followed by Edwin "Buzz" Aldrin, planned to exit the lunar module and set the first human steps on the moon. From approximately 240,000 miles away, Mae could watch this mind-boggling feat happen after only a few seconds of delay.

The image on the television was grainy and in black and white. Despite the shadowy quality of the picture, Mae could make out Neil descending a ladder from the lunar module. His spacesuit was bulky and his movements slow. She wondered, *What will happen when he steps on the moon?*

At first Neil kept his hands on the ladder. The surface, he described over a scratchy radio transmission, was made up of a very fine powder. He kicked some of it up with his boot. Then, when he stepped away from the ladder, his famous words rang in Mae's ears. "That's one small step for man, one giant leap for mankind."

Yes! Mae thought to herself. *That's what* I'm *going to do.* No matter the obstacles or difficulties, Mae vowed that someday she, too, would travel to space. She took it a step further than the moon, however. Mae figured that by the time she was grown up, she would be a scientist working on Mars.

Space Race

When Neil Armstrong and Buzz Aldrin walked on the moon, nobody had ever made a call from a handheld cellphone. People didn't have computers in their homes, and gas cost 35 cents a gallon. Meanwhile NASA—the National Aeronautics and Space Administration—had been created a decade earlier and was using cutting-edge technology to win the "Space Race." This was an unofficial contest between the United States and the Soviet Union to succeed at space exploration. Both governments were determined to prove their technological superiority in space.

At first, the Soviets seemed to be ahead when, on October 4, 1957, they launched the first ever satellite, which they called Sputnik. Soviet scientists soon deployed Sputnik 2, this time with a dog named Laika onboard. The United States followed, but instead of a dog, they launched two primates into space. Soon, the first human in space was Yuri Gagarin. The USSR scientists gained another victory when they sent him to orbit around the Earth. Achieving a similar milestone less than a month later, Alan Shepard became the first American in space. The first woman in space was Soviet Valentina Tereshkova. As the two countries jockeyed to be first in the race to conquer space, the United States launched the rocket ship Apollo 11. With the success of landing the first human beings on the moon, the United States won a major victory in the Space Race.

Mae Jemison was born on October 17, 1956, just as the world's interest in conquering space accelerated. Smart and precocious, Mae decided early on that she wanted to be a scientist and made that announcement in her kindergarten class. "Don't you mean a nurse?" her teacher asked her.

No. Mae was certain it was a scientist, not a nurse, that she wanted to become. Despite her teacher's comment and despite the fact that she was a girl, Mae was determined to achieve her goal. At the time, most scientists were men. Never mind that she was also African American and that there were fewer opportunities in the sciences for people of color. However, Mae wasn't going to let unfair obstacles stand in her way.

Mae spent her childhood exploring, learning, and dancing. She loved watching *Star Trek* and finding out about science. If she didn't understand something, she would check out books from the library and study them until she figured it out. She wasn't afraid to ask questions, either. *How did life evolve on our planet?* she asked herself in elementary school. In response, she researched answers and built an elaborate diorama to represent the Earth's different eras.

One day, Mae's mother asked her a question: "What is sickle cell anemia?" By now a high school junior, Mae met the challenge by calling up the local hospital, and, after explaining that she was working on a science project, she began volunteering in the hospital's hematology lab to find out more.

Not surprisingly, Mae completed high school early. After skipping seventh grade, she was awarded a scholarship to Stanford University at age 16. Never having visited the campus or even been to California before, Mae was wearing a homemade jacket when she boarded an airplane headed to San Francisco. Her suitcase was full of more self-made clothes—she liked the better-quality material, and besides, homemade clothes were much cheaper than the ones in stores. Mae's heart was full of excitement, but also worry. Would her parents be okay without her? As the plane banked left, Mae got her first view of Stanford, a series of red tiled roofs.

The next few years were busy and eye-opening. Not all of the Stanford professors welcomed Mae onto campus. When Mae wanted to continue her study of Russian, despite four years of learning the language in high school, she was told that she'd have to start from scratch. She enrolled in Swahili instead.

Mae, determined to succeed no matter what, focused on her academics, and, four years later, she earned a Bachelor of Science degree in chemical engineering. She had also completed enough credits for an undergraduate degree in African and Afro-American Studies. But Mae wasn't done. Now it was time for medical school.

This time, Mae's schooling took her to the opposite side of the continent. She enrolled in Cornell University Medical College in New York City and began classes there in the fall of 1977. While Mae was getting used to her new routine, new roommate, and new selection of courses, other classmates were initially two steps ahead. Mae hadn't thought to prepare ahead of time. On the first day of classes, when Mae expected to sit through lectures and ease into things, her professor instructed the students to get ready for a dissection. Mae was assigned to a group and to a cadaver—a dead human body.

Already? Mae followed her classmates to the lab. While the other students seemed eager to peel back skin and tissue so they could learn and explore, Mae felt slightly queasy—she was glad to let someone else do the cutting. Not only that, but the other students had also studied beforehand and already knew the Latin names of the muscles, organs, blood vessels, bones, and nerves. Mae quickly realized that she was going to have to put aside all squeamishness and catch up.

Medical school was much more intense than Stanford. Mae poured herself into her studies, and soon she not only caught up but also excelled. Putting her initial discomfort aside, she found what she was doing to be fascinating, eventually finding even the hands-on dissection class interesting. But there was always a lot to learn. Mae often snatched only a few hours of sleep in between studying, especially before exams.

Despite her grueling schedule, Mae remained active in other areas of her life. She enrolled in dance classes, played occasional basketball, and explored what New York City had to offer whenever she had a few free minutes. She also joined clubs and took on leadership positions. Over the summers, she traveled to Cuba and Kenya to work with medical study groups and then to Thailand to work in a Cambodian refugee camp. It was amazing that she had any time to sleep at all.

When Mae graduated, she knew she wanted to travel and to help people all over the world. The idea of visiting space still tugged at her, too. First, though, she completed an internship and then worked for a short time as a doctor in California. She then took a job with the US Peace Corps and served overseas again, this time in Sierra Leone and Liberia. When Mae came back to the United States in 1985, she applied to NASA's astronaut program. Initially, a terrible disaster derailed her plan.

The *Challenger*: Catastrophic Failure

Despite the meticulous planning and countless hours of cross-checking and careful calculations, the unbelievable happened shortly after liftoff of the space shuttle *Challenger* on January 28, 1986. The shuttle's booster rockets consisted of four fuel segments. When a rubber seal between the segments failed due to the unusually cold temperature outside, it caused a chain reaction. Cameras were broadcasting on live TV as the shuttle blew apart. All seven astronauts on board perished. Among the crewmembers was teacher Christa McAuliffe. The first educator in the newly formed "Teacher in Space" program, Christa had been chosen out of approximately 11,000 applicants. She had planned to transmit lessons from space back to Earth. One of the lessons she planned to share was called "The Ultimate Field Trip." The tragic loss of the *Challenger* caused a major setback for NASA's space program, and it would be another two years before NASA attempted another mission into space.

As news of the *Challenger* tragedy reverberated throughout the country and the world, Mae's aspiration to journey to space was put on hold. She knew that the mission was as important as ever, however, and as soon as NASA was open to applications two years later, she applied to the astronaut program again. This time, one of 15 out of 2,000, she was accepted. She was the first African American woman admitted into the training. Five years later, she became the first woman of color—in the *world*—to travel to space.

Mae was one of seven crewmembers onboard the space shuttle *Endeavor*. Space Transportation System (STS)-47 Spacelab J was a cooperative mission between the United States and Japan. Because of this, there was a Japanese astronaut along, too. In addition to going on the mission itself, Mae was excited to practice her Japanese—she had taught herself the language in anticipation of the assignment.

The *Endeavor* launched on September 12, 1992. After surviving the shaking and rattling of the shuttle's trajectory off-planet, Mae experienced her first view of Earth. It was a direct line over Chicago, her beloved hometown. The sight brought her an intense sense of belonging. Later she commented, "I'm as much a part of this universe as any speck of stardust."

STS-47 was Mae's only trip to space. She and the other crewmembers spent 190 hours, 30 minutes, and 23 seconds orbiting the Earth 126 times. Mae worked as a science mission specialist conducting experiments, including bone cell research. The data was important because it helped people understand the consequences of living in space.

When Mae finished her mission in space, she didn't pause or even slow down. Initially, she took a teaching job after retiring from NASA shortly after her space experience. She founded her own company, the Jemison Group, to encourage the creation of some of the world's most cutting-edge technology, especially to help those in the developing world. She also formed the Dorothy Jemison Foundation for Excellence, named in honor of her mother who had always encouraged her to ask questions. The company's mission is to foster the same enthusiasm and curiosity for the world in young people as Mae feels herself. Part of the foundation's outreach includes a summer camp called The Earth We Share (TEWS) where kids ages 12 to 16 are encouraged to think and solve problems in various science fields.

Along with these new opportunities, something else special happened when Mae first came back to Earth. Her love of *Star Trek* reached the ears of Hollywood powerhouse LeVar Burton. When he reached out to Mae to ask if she would be willing to appear on a *Star Trek* episode, she jumped at the chance. Mae played Lieutenant Palmer on the 1993 episode titled "Second Chances." Nichelle Nichols, the actress who played Lieutenant Uhura and who inspired Mae when she was a girl, came to visit Mae on the set. It was a moment in Mae's life when she felt like she'd come full circle.

Life on Other Planets? Myth or Maybe?

Exoplanets are those planets that are outside our solar system. Is there life on any of these worlds? According to scientists, the answer is . . . maybe. But if there is, how are we going to find out? The James Webb Space Telescope (JWST) is part of a recent project to study the mysteries of the universe. Fourteen countries contributed to its construction. Unlike the Hubble telescope that orbits Earth, JWST is built to orbit the sun approximately 1.5 million miles away from Earth. It is 100 times more powerful than the Hubble, too. Part of the JWST mission is to locate planets that are conducive to sustaining life. According to NASA scientist Dr. Ravi Kumar Kopparapu, "It's not a question of 'if,' it's a question of 'when' we find life on other planets."

Today, one of Mae's greatest contributions is her involvement in a project called the 100-Year Starship (100YSS). Originally, the Defense Advanced Research Projects Agency (DARPA) launched an initiative to prepare for interstellar travel. The objective was to develop a forum that would pave the way for interstellar space travel within a period of 100 years. Mae now leads this organization. While she supervises advances in technology that will be critical for future interstellar travel, she also oversees developments that benefit current conditions on Earth. The 100YSS project claims, "We believe that pursuing an extraordinary tomorrow will build a better world today."

Building a spaceship that can travel throughout the universe is an enormous undertaking that, to some, seems impossible. But Mae has a quick answer for the naysayers. She reminds us, "If you think about it, H. G. Wells wrote *First*

Men in the Moon in 1901. Imagine how incredulous, fantastical that idea was in 1901. We didn't have rockets, we didn't have the materials, and we weren't really flying. It was incredible. Less than 100 years later, we were on the moon."

Throughout her life, Mae has faced significant hurdles in her pursuit to become an astronaut and Earth advocate. The path she chose involved intense and very hard work. There were several points where, had she slacked off even a little, she would not have succeeded. There were other times when what she did was dangerous. For example, in 2003, the *Columbia* was the second space shuttle to malfunction. It disintegrated as it was reentering Earth's atmosphere, again killing all seven crewmembers onboard. This disaster—and others—underscores the dangers of space exploration, though Mae knows it's worth the risks.

Today Mae is at the forefront of advancing space exploration for humans while helping improve life here on Earth. She points out, "Never be limited by others' limited imaginations; never limit others because of your own limited imagination."

But will Mae see the launch of a viable spaceship capable of traveling far distances in her own lifetime? She isn't sure. However, she *is* certain that her work now will be one giant leap for humankind toward this next exploration milestone. Perhaps *Star Trek* will not be so far-fetched then.

Follow Mae Jemison Online

Website: www.drmae.com

Instagram: @therealmaejemison

Twitter: @maejemison

Facebook: 100 Year Starship

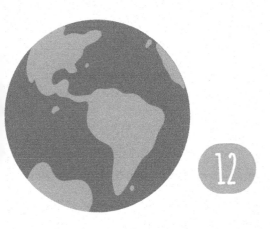

Ellen Ochoa:
Music Amongst the Stars

"T-minus 20 seconds."

The voice from Mission Control at the Kennedy Space Center in Florida sounded calm and clear inside the space shuttle *Discovery*. As Ellen Ochoa sat secured to her seat in the orbiter, she didn't have time to think about the enormity of the moment. She just hoped they would be able to launch this time. Two days before, the liftoff had been scrubbed a mere 11 seconds before they were scheduled to initiate the launch sequence. Now, on April 8, 1993, it seemed like everything was working properly and that mission STS-56 would go ahead as scheduled.

"We have a go for engine start." The countdown continued as Ellen braced herself for the launch of the 4.5 million–pound system into space.

"We have ignition. We have liftoff of *Discovery* on the second mission to Planet Earth Research Flight."

It was 1:29 in the morning when the *Discovery* finally fired for launch. Ellen was fully outfitted in her astronaut flight suit, the visor on her helmet down and locked. Despite all her preparation, it was hard to imagine the staggering power needed to thrust the crew of five and their vehicle into space, but the rumbling and vibration inside the shuttle gave her a hint. The spacecraft seemed almost alive as it climbed higher. *It's happening. It's actually happening,* Ellen told herself.

At two minutes after liftoff, the shuttle was approximately 30 miles (45 km) above the launch pad. No longer needed, two booster rockets detached from the orbiter and fell back to Earth. Ellen knew they would splash harmlessly into the ocean where a NASA team would recover them to be refurbished for another shuttle mission.

The next part of the launch happened precisely as Ellen anticipated, too. At five minutes, the *Discovery* was traveling at 7,000 miles an hour—and accelerating. After an intense eight and a half minutes, the external fuel tank separated from the spacecraft. Unlike the orbiter and the twin rocket boosters, this external tank was built for one use only. Now empty, the detached tank fell back toward Earth and burned up as it reentered the Earth's atmosphere. Ellen assured herself that the *Discovery* had over 27,000 heat resistant tiles on its exterior to ensure that the same thing did *not* happen to them.

No longer pinned by gravity, anything not tied down now floated around the flight deck. It would be a little over nine days and 3.9 million miles before Ellen felt the effects of the Earth's pull again. When she and the crew did return home, they would glide down to the Earth's surface like a plane—*if* all went as planned. Of course, traveling to space was an enormous undertaking where everything had to go exactly right. If anything went wrong . . . well, there had been tragedies.

Ellen didn't focus on the danger of the mission. To her, the opportunity to leave Earth's atmosphere far outweighed any potential catastrophe. She told herself, *I've got a job to do, and I need to do it right.*

Space Transportation System (STS)

The first human-involved flights into space were with one-use-only rocket ships. Only the tip of the rocket, a small capsule to hold the crew, made it back to Earth. The United States developed a next generation of spacecrafts that could be reused multiple times. These were the Space Transportation Systems (STS), commonly known as space shuttles. There were five shuttles in the program: *Columbia, Challenger, Discovery, Atlantis,* and *Endeavour.* An additional shuttle named *Enterprise* was used only for testing and never left the atmosphere.

On April 12, 1981, *Columbia* was the first shuttle to launch into orbit, where it stayed for over two days. Flying at 17,500 miles per hour meant that the crew inside experienced a sunrise or sunset every 45 minutes. Upon reentry into the Earth's atmosphere, the shuttle didn't splash down via parachute into the ocean like previous spacecraft. Instead, it dropped landing gear and glided to solid earth.

Though she was born in Los Angeles, Ellen grew up near San Diego, one of five children. After her parents divorced, Ellen watched her mother work hard to raise the family. This work ethic rubbed off on Ellen—success, she saw, was the result of determined effort. Still, she never dreamed that someday she would play such an important role in the space program.

Like the rest of the world, Ellen was fascinated when she watched the TV broadcast of the first men walking on the moon. The space program was exciting, but it didn't occur to 11-year-old Ellen that she could someday take part in it, too. She couldn't imagine that she would be the first Latina to travel to space. The only people she saw involved were men, and to Ellen, it didn't seem like that was going to change. But what *would* she do? She wasn't sure.

Ellen grew up reading, especially books where there was a female protagonist. *A Wrinkle in Time* was one of her favorites. She began practicing the flute when she was 10. When she joined various bands—the honor band, the marching band, and others—it instilled in her a sense of teamwork. Each member of a band contributed to the music. Academically, Ellen did well, too. Really well. She loved math and calculus in particular. She was valedictorian at Grossmont High School in La Mesa, California.

Ellen needed to decide what to do after high school. While she had been offered a small scholarship for Stanford University, it didn't come close to covering the cost of going to school there. Instead, she chose to stay home and enrolled at San Diego State University. But Ellen wasn't sure what she wanted to study. She considered journalism or business or maybe even music—she was still passionate about playing the flute. She finally settled on physics, and in 1980, she earned her bachelor's degree. Once again, she was valedictorian of her graduating class.

Ellen wasn't done with school. She knew she wanted to continue studying, so when Stanford University offered her a fellowship that would help pay for her graduate studies, she quickly accepted. This time Ellen focused on electrical engineering for a master's and then doctorate degree. She did research work in the field of optics, helping computers identify images more precisely. It was during grad school that Ellen first heard of astronaut Sally Ride.

Sally and Ellen had a few things in common. Like Ellen, Sally had gone to Stanford. She had also majored in physics.

Ellen wondered . . . could *she* apply to be an astronaut, too? By now NASA was accepting female astronaut candidates. Plus, they were looking for scientists and researchers to travel to space, no longer just pilots. When some of Ellen's friends applied to the astronaut program, she decided to put in her application, too.

Sally Ride Leads the Way

In 1963, Valentina Tereshkova, a cosmonaut from the Soviet Union, was the first woman in space. Almost exactly 20 years later, on June 18, 1983, Dr. Sally Ride became the first American woman in space. Like Ellen Ochoa, when Sally was younger it didn't occur to her that she could be an astronaut. She was excellent at tennis, and for a while, she considered a professional career in the sport. Her life took a different turn. One day while earning her advanced degree from Stanford University, Sally saw an advertisement from NASA calling for female applicants. She applied with 8,000 others and was one of six women chosen. Sally completed two missions to space, but her third assignment was cancelled after the *Challenger* exploded soon after liftoff. Sally spent her life advocating for women in science. Sadly, she died from cancer at just 61 years old. After her death, President Obama awarded her the Presidential Medal of Freedom. He said at the ceremony, "As the first American woman in space, Sally did not just break the stratospheric glass ceiling, she blasted through it."

As Ellen began her career as an engineer at Sandia National Laboratories, she applied to NASA's astronaut program—but didn't get in. Instead of giving up, Ellen earned her private pilot's license. It wouldn't hurt to have that credential if, or rather *when*, she tried again.

Ellen applied once more to become a NASA astronaut. This time, she was one of 100 finalists. Then, in 1990, she got a phone call. She had been accepted into the astronaut candidate program! She sat back and thought about what that meant. *It's one of those moments in your life where you know your life is going to change forever.*

Now that Ellen was part of the program, she was considered an astronaut candidate until she finished her first year of training. The year of instruction and practice was like being in school again, only here there was an even greater mountain of information to learn. Ellen, along with 22 others in her class, was given a stack of workbooks. But the academics were no problem—Ellen was used to book learning. It was the operational requirements of her new job that at first made her worry.

The astronaut program included a ton of hands-on learning. The candidates practiced on life-size models of the space shuttle's systems, called mock-ups. Ellen became an expert on how to operate everything inside the spacecraft. Simulations not only prepared her to function in space but also tested her ability to solve potential problems that could derail the mission—or worse. Each astronaut candidate was put in high-stress situations to test his or her ability to make rational decisions and stay calm.

Part of Ellen's training involved flying in the backseat of a T-38 jet. These high-performing planes provided an excellent opportunity for real-life experience. Ellen learned how to focus on the critical components of a situation and prioritize what was most important. It was a fast-moving environment that was both thrilling and sobering, a reminder of how harsh life was outside the Earth's atmosphere.

Part of space flight preparation included survival training, too. Ellen had no background in this aspect of the training. She had never even been a girl scout! As Ellen spent time in a remote location where she and her crewmates devised a tent using the material from a parachute, she worked on various land survival skills. Despite her initial lack of knowledge, Ellen was acutely aware of one thing. Rehearsing for potential problems now would better her chances for making the right decisions while in space.

Ellen also learned how to eject out of an aircraft. She parachuted into the ocean and had to figure out how to haul herself into a raft on a choppy sea. She also learned how to scuba dive so she could participate in spacewalk training in a giant pool.

There the sensation of being underwater had certain similar characteristics to the microgravity of space. To further simulate weightlessness outside the Earth's atmosphere, Ellen and her teammates flew in an airplane not-so-affectionately nicknamed the "Vomit Comet."

NASA used a KC-135 Stratotanker to create an artificial weightless atmosphere. By having the plane fly in an inverted "U" shape, the astronaut candidates could experience approximately 25 seconds of zero gravity each time the plane reached its peak altitude and then dipped back down. Ellen and the others were given specific tasks to perform during this 25-second period. For example, sometimes she practiced eating or manipulating tools. It was disconcerting and difficult, but also kind of fun once she got used to the feeling.

Finally, the candidate classes were over. NASA deemed Ellen ready to launch as a full-fledged astronaut. Ellen felt ready, too. But when she was assigned to her first mission in 1993, she hoped she would remember everything she needed to do.

The *Discovery*'s STS-56 mission had several components. Ellen's job as a mission specialist included operating a robotic arm as well as conducting scientific experiments. Several instruments for measuring the sun's impact on the Earth's atmosphere had been brought aboard. Scientists back home would use the data to measure and study the Earth's ozone layer. The assignment included launching a free-flying satellite that would measure solar wind as well as the sun's corona—the sun's atmosphere. All eyes were on Ellen as she manipulated the shuttle's robotic arm to place the satellite in space and then retrieve it several days later.

Throughout the flight, there was almost no time—or room—for anything besides the mission. However, along with the scientific equipment, there was another instrument aboard, this one personal. In between her designated tasks, Ellen was allowed to squeeze in time to play her beloved flute as part of an educational video for children. It was a historic first, and Ellen happily shared the experience with the people back on Earth.

Finally, after 9 days, 6 hours, 8 minutes, and 24 seconds—not to mention 148 orbits around the planet—Ellen and the rest of the crew landed safely back on Earth. The data they brought with them was invaluable. But there wasn't time to slow down and savor the accomplishment. A mere year and a half later, Ellen went on her second journey to space, this time on the *Atlantis* space shuttle. For this second space assignment, she was the payload commander, the person who oversaw the management of all the experiments to be conducted. She helped collect more data from the sun and atmosphere, important in the study of the ozone layer. But that wasn't all. Ellen still had two more space assignments to complete.

Mission STS-96 had a different purpose than Ellen's previous two flights. This time, she would fly in the *Discovery* again, but she and her crewmates would help construct the new International Space Station (ISS). As one of the leaders in this endeavor, Ellen had worked for years to develop a plan for how international crews would use the outpost built in space. Part of this preparation had involved flying to Russia to tour the soon-to-be-launched Russian section of the station. Later, when it was operating in space, everything seemed familiar when she stepped inside.

Since the ISS was constructed in space, each section of it was transported up, piece by piece. While they were the second shuttle mission to help with the assembly of the ISS, Ellen and her team were the first to dock a shuttle onto the so far unmanned station. When STS-96 arrived, there was only one solar array—part of the Russian module—to power the whole station, which didn't yet have the capacity to support a live-in crew. That would come later—for now Ellen and her team were tasked with getting things ready.

Ellen's final trip to space was with the space shuttle *Atlantis*. Again, her crew's purpose was to help construct the ISS. By now, teams of people were living aboard the science outpost, monitoring the functions of the station and conducting experiments. The payload bay of the *Atlantis* carried a 40-foot truss, a structural support framework Ellen's crew would attach to the exterior of the station. It was Ellen's job to use the robotic arm to lift it out of the shuttle and position it so that two other crewmembers could perform spacewalks to finish the installation.

The International Space Station

The ISS is a multinational, collaborative project to further scientific research. Since April 2021, participants from 19 countries have inhabited the space station, including commercial space travelers who pay millions of dollars each to participate. The largest proportion of astronauts and space participants have come from the United States, followed by Russia and then Japan. The ISS travels at 300 miles per minute and is in orbit at an average altitude of 250 miles above the Earth's surface. Up until recently, crews of six lived aboard the station for months at a time—now that number has risen to seven crewmembers. In 2007, Peggy Whitson became the station's first female commander. She has spent an incredible total of 665 days in the ISS.

After her fourth and final flight, Ellen landed at the Kennedy Space Center located at Cape Canaveral, Florida. All told, she had spent nearly 1,000 hours in space. With her talent and experience, Ellen moved into other leadership positions within NASA including a six-year tenure as director of the Lyndon B. Johnson Space Center in Houston, Texas. She was the first Latinx person and second female in that role.

Ellen's legacy is impressive and far-reaching. Her impact on the world and on space exploration is hard to quantify. To date, she has six schools named after her and has had various books and publications written about her. Earning award after award, she continues to encourage and inspire young people with talks and appearances around the country. What she tells her audiences over and over is this: "What everyone in the astronaut corps shares in common is not gender or ethnic background, but motivation, perseverance, and desire—the desire to participate in a voyage of discovery."

According to Ellen, our mission to explore space has barely begun.

Follow Ellen Ochoa Online

Website: https://ellenochoa.space/

Instagram: @ellen_ochoa

Twitter: @Astro_Ellen

Samantha Cristoforetti: Home in Space

The Neutral Buoyancy Laboratory (NBL) is located in the Sonny Carter Training Facility near the Johnson Space Center in Houston, Texas. The NBL is essentially a giant pool of water—it measures over 200 feet (61 m) long, 100 feet (30 m) wide, and 40 feet (12 m) deep. Submerged in this gigantic 6.2-million-gallon facility is a full-scale replica of several components of the International Space Station (ISS). Astronauts from around the world train at the NBL to prepare for spacewalks—NASA calls these extravehicular activities or EVAs. Today, Italy's first female astronaut, Samantha Cristoforetti, was about to experience a simulated EVA.

Excited to get started, Samantha had been looking forward to this exercise for months. While conditions underwater aren't the same as being in the microgravity of space, they provide a close and helpful approximation. To her, the NBL training was one step closer to experiencing the real thing. Like space, though, Samantha knew that the training could be dangerous. Although she had done trail runs using scuba gear, she had never been underwater wearing the approximately 280-pound suit known as an extravehicular mobility unit or EMU. If something went wrong—unlikely, but it could happen—it would take precious minutes before she was hauled from the water and the suit was removed.

Well, that's why there's a team of medical professionals and equipment standing by, she reminded herself.

Preparation for today's training had started a couple of months ago. Samantha had come to the facility to meet with a suit engineer, the person responsible for prepping the high-tech outfit she'd be wearing today. The process had taken hours. Since EMUs aren't custom-made for each astronaut, the suit engineer performed more than 80 different measurements of Samantha's body to determine the correct torso, legs, boots, arms, and gloves to use for her. He took 23 measurements of her hands alone. Finding the right gloves had been tricky, but Samantha was glad that the engineer had taken his time. When assigned a real spacewalk, Samantha would need to be able to hold and manipulate various tools, so proper fit was critical.

This morning, Samantha had arrived early. Suiting up was a long and painstaking process, though it seemed that the scientists had thought of everything. First, since she would be underwater for hours, she put on a MAG—a maximum absorbency garment (a diaper made for an adult). Samantha dressed in a set of long-sleeved underwear and leggings to protect her skin from rubbing against the next layer, the Liquid Cooling and Ventilation Garment, or LCVG. This close-fitting device included over 230 feet (70 m) of tubing to carry cooling water across her body. While Samantha wasn't feeling too hot or too cold right now, she knew that she would appreciate the temperature regulating device once she was inside the suit and underwater.

Technicians placed the outer shell of the suit over Samantha's torso. Next, they sealed on the leg pieces at her waist. After the helmet and gloves went on, they secured a mini workstation, a rack for tools, to the front of her suit. This placement gave her easy access to the things she would need for the mission.

By now, Samantha was nervous, but she reassured herself that everyone knew what they were doing. A team would be monitoring everything she did, including two safety divers who would swim next to her throughout the exercise. Besides, she told herself, she had been preparing for this for months. Of course, practicing with diving equipment was vastly different from working in a suit designed for space.

Samantha stood on a platform over the water. It was attached to a crane because by now, Samantha's body, suit, and tools weighed several hundred pounds. Once she was lowered underwater, the safety divers would add more weights to her suit. These were carefully calibrated so that she would be neutrally buoyant—she would neither sink nor rise. Samantha tensed as the crane lowered her into the pool. This was it!

Extravehicular Activity—EVA

The first person to conduct an EVA was Russia's Alexei Leonov on March 18, 1965. He left his space capsule to spend over 12 minutes in space. A few months later, on June 3, 1965, Ed White was the first American to exit his spacecraft to float in space. Attached to a gold-plated tether that also fed him oxygen, his EVA lasted 23 minutes. "It's the saddest moment of my life," he reportedly said when ordered back inside.

The first woman to experience an EVA was Soviet cosmonaut Svetlana Savitskaya in 1984, followed by US astronaut Kathryn Sullivan that same year. Also in 1984, Bruce McCandless II took things a step further when he exited his spacecraft without a tether. Instead, he used a nitrogen-propelled device called a Manned Maneuvering Unit. Another important milestone in the history of spaceflight was when Christina Koch and Jessica Meir conducted the first all-female spacewalk in 2019.

Samantha Cristoforetti has always been fascinated with space. Born in Milan, Italy, on April 26, 1977, she grew up in a small mountain village in the Italian Alps. Taught to read at a young age by her grandmother, Samantha loved books, especially science fiction. Plus, since there was very little light pollution above her home, she often gazed at the night sky and thought about how amazing it would be to someday travel outside Earth's limit. Still, traveling to space herself seemed like an impossible dream.

Samantha loved adventure. Her parents ran a hotel in the village, which meant that during the busy seasons of winter and summer, tourists brought their kids, and Samantha had a steady stream of new playmates. Together they explored the outdoors, satisfying Samantha's curiosity and her need to discover. Great early teachers also stoked Samantha's pioneering spirit. It's not surprising that when she was in high school, she embraced the opportunity to study abroad. She chose the United States.

Samantha was drawn to the United States for many reasons. First, it was the birthplace of *Star Trek* and also NASA. It also gave her the chance to develop her English language capacity and to learn something of the culture she'd heard so much about. Samantha spent a year in St. Paul, Minnesota, before returning to Italy for her final year of high school.

Now Samantha had another decision to make. She knew she was going to go to college, but what should she study? She settled on engineering and once again decided to experience the language and culture of another country.

Samantha studied aeronautical sciences in Germany at the University of Munich. While there, she set her sights on Russia, another country deeply invested in the quest to explore space. Was there a way to finish her studies as an exchange student there?

Lucky for Samantha, one of her professors had a connection to the Mendeleev University in Moscow. During her 11 months there, as Samantha was finishing her bachelor's degree, another opportunity arose. The Italian government announced a monumental change in the country's air force. In the year 2000, females would finally be accepted into the program. Though it meant starting over with another undergraduate degree, Samantha applied to the *Accademia Aeronautica*, the Italian Air Force Academy, ultimately coming in first in the admissions competition process.

After graduating from the Italian Air Force, Samantha was sent to Sheppard Air Force Base in Texas. Here she earned her pilot wings, the certification to fly. Now she went back to Italy and underwent a whirlwind qualification process to fly the AM-X ground attack fighter plane. Unexpectedly, another chance event came along.

For the first time in 15 years, the European Space Agency (ESA) put out a call for astronaut applications. Unlike NASA, which accepts new astronaut candidates on a regular basis, the ESA's program is much smaller, and they infrequently take on new astronauts. Despite her intense schedule, Samantha knew it might be her one and only chance to apply. She sent in her paperwork.

When Samantha made the first cut in Europe's Space Program selection process, there were still 1,000 other potential candidates out of an initial 8,400 applicants. Then, after more tests and interviews, the committee whittled the group down to 192 people, then 45, then 22. Ultimately, in 2009, Samantha was finally chosen as one of 6 ESA astronauts. Now the real work of how to prepare for space was going to begin.

Samantha's new class of astronauts named themselves the Shenanigans and immersed themselves in training. The next few years included book learning, medical training, simulations, and practice using a mock-up of the International Space Station's robotic arm. Though there was no guarantee that she would ever perform a spacewalk, Samantha rehearsed vigorously for the possibility—hoping fervently that she would someday get the opportunity. It would be nearly five years before Samantha was assigned a mission in space.

Meanwhile, the work to becoming an astronaut involved travel to Canada, the United States, Russia, and Japan—each time for specific exercises and drills. Aside from learning about systems and various procedures, Samantha and her teammates practiced what to do if things went wrong. The scenarios tested her knowledge as well as gauged how she would react under stress. She participated in survival exercises including one in the Sardinian highlands and another in a Russian forest.

Analog Missions

Today, NASA is actively preparing for future space missions beyond Earth's low orbit. There are plans for exploration to Mars, to the moon, and to nearby asteroids. To get ready for these endeavors, NASA conducts analog missions—field tests—at various remote locations on Earth. Analog missions provide a practical, quicker, and less expensive opportunity to test technology, robotics, various systems, habitats, and human concerns on Earth before going into space. For example, NASA's Human Exploration Research Analog (HERA) tests the human effects of isolation and confinement. Human test subjects volunteer to spend weeks in a small, windowless habitat. Another analog site is the Haughton-Mars Project (HMP) found on Devon Island in British Columbia, Canada. The location with its isolation, cold temperatures, and dry, barren landscape is ideal for Mars and moon simulation experiments. Analog missions are a valuable opportunity to prepare for deep space exploration.

Samantha's time finally came. On November 23, 2014, she was at the Baikonur Cosmodrome in Kazakhstan, hours away from liftoff. Her assignment was flight engineer for Expedition 42/43. The mission, called Futura, would involve 200 days aboard the International Space Station. In just a few hours,

Samantha, along with two crewmates, commander Anton Shkaplerov and flight engineer Terry Virts, would fly aboard a Russian rocket on the six-hour journey to dock at the low-orbiting outpost.

After taking a mandatory pre-launch nap, Samantha ran through everything she'd done to prepare for this moment. She had bags packed for when she arrived back on Earth in several months' time since she'd be immediately whisked off to Houston after landing. She had composed an automatic email reply message that read: "I'll be off planet for a while, back in May 2015. Unfortunately I won't read your message." She'd also taken her last shower for months—there was no running water on the ISS. Was there anything else she had forgotten to take care of?

Hours later, Samantha climbed through the access hatch into the cramped cockpit of the Soyuz, the orbital module on top of a Russian rocket. She slid into her seat and attached the various systems—communication, oxygen, ventilation, medical monitors—and waited as a technician strapped her in. Next came a lengthy process of checks. At 10 minutes to launch, Samantha lowered the visor of her helmet, making sure it was properly sealed.

"We are GO for launch."

One minute and 14 seconds after midnight, the crew achieved liftoff. Each stage was accompanied by noise, jolts, and vibrations. About 100 miles (160 kilometers) above the

Earth's surface, the spacecraft reached orbit. With a successful launch behind them, the next phase of the journey was to dock with the ISS, 1,900 miles (3,000 km) in front of them.

The Soyuz

Pronounced SAW-yooz, for years, this Russian spacecraft was the primary means of transporting international astronauts along with Russian cosmonauts to the ISS. But this space vehicle was in existence long before the ISS.

The first Soyuz launched on November 28, 1966. Since then, this reliable spacecraft has completed hundreds of trips to space, sometimes to deliver food and supplies and other times to replace the crew aboard the ISS. Inside the capsule, located on top of a rocket, there is room for three cosmonauts and astronauts. It takes six hours to get to the space station, but only three and a half hours to return to Earth. The return trip, as many have testified, is a bumpy ride. Today, space agencies have other, commercial options for travel to space.

When the Soyuz arrived at the ISS, an automatic docking system was put into place, all captured on camera and broadcast back to Earth. Finally, after two hours of checking for leaking seals, the crew opened the hatch for the ISS. Anton offered

Samantha the chance to enter first, and, as she floated forward, she became the 216th person to visit the ISS.

Samantha's first moments inside the station seemed surreal, but also comfortingly familiar. The mock-ups and simulations on Earth were close replicas to the reality of the station here. From the tools and implements Velcroed to the walls, to the packets of warmed up food, and especially to a porthole showing the Earth, this was Samantha's new temporary home.

At first, moving around was clumsy and disorienting. Early in her stay, Samantha was sorting through a box of drink packets—she desperately wanted some black coffee—when some of the other packets started floating away. In her hasty attempt to guide them back into their container, she accidently did a flip and was upside down—not that direction mattered. It would take some time before Samantha was able to anchor every move.

Samantha's work on the space station settled into a regimented and busy schedule, or as close to a schedule as possible given the unique and incredible circumstances. Each workday started and ended with a Daily Planning Conference (DPC) where the crew coordinated with their earthbound counterparts. Samantha's day was divided into increments with the day's tasks clearly outlined. Next the crew went through a checklist of emergency procedures where they tested various components and systems in the station. While computers helped monitor how everything was working, Samantha and the others also executed a number of hands-on assessments. A large portion of her time, however, was spent on experiments.

One aspect of Samantha's work was to collect data on how the human body responds to space. She helped collect data on biological functions and the effects of space radiation on her body. Back home on Earth, scientists could analyze this information to help with future space travel as well as work on improving conditions on Earth.

There was another critical component to each day: exercise. Since weightlessness leads to loss of bone density and muscle tissue, all ISS astronauts are required to work out every day. The station includes gym equipment such as a modified treadmill, exercise bike, and weight-lifting machine. When Samantha tethered herself to the treadmill, she entertained herself by watching *Battlestar Galactica* episodes while running in space.

The Saturday routine was a little different. This was the day when the crew conducted household chores. It was easy for the living areas to become messy or disorganized. Samantha helped vacuum filters, clean up, and do repairs. For example, it seemed like the toilet broke down frequently. With limited tools and equipment aboard, sometimes fixing things required creative problem-solving.

Not every day was predictable. There were often other jobs to do such as unloading cargo from unmanned supply ships or perhaps launching a satellite that had been transported into orbit. There were also spacewalks to conduct repairs on the outside of the station, though Samantha's role this time was to assist inside the ISS. There was contact with school groups and other organizations. Finally, limited time was set aside to communicate with friends and family on Earth.

Too soon, it was time for reentry into Earth's atmosphere. On June 11, 2015, Samantha and her crewmates spent hectic last hours preparing to leave the station. By the time she crammed into the Soyuz descent module and touched down on Earth, Samantha had spent nearly 200 days in space.

The experience in the ISS changed Samantha. She appreciated precious Earth more than ever and vowed to take care of it. She also knew that she wasn't done with the European Space Agency. After participating in post-mission activities and adapting back to the conditions of Earth—including strengthening her weakened muscles from being in space so long—she reacquainted herself with her family and then eased back into work.

With an eye on future missions to the moon, Samantha worked from the European Space Agency located in Cologne, Germany. She continued to spend time in Star City and at NASA as well. She made history again when she participated in the first cooperative training mission between Chinese and non-Chinese astronauts. In between everything, she wrote a book, *Diary of an Apprentice Astronaut*, and donated the royalties to charity.

Samantha reflects on her view of Earth from space. "When you look at the Earth from space, it looks like a big space ship that is flying through space, and oh, by the way, carrying all of humanity on it. And so you start to get this feeling that, just as on the space station, we can only function if we all work together as a crew and we're all crew members."

Follow Samantha Cristoforetti Online

Website: https://blogs.esa.int/exploration/category /astronauts/samantha-cristoforetti/

Instagram: @Samantha_Cristoforetti

Twitter: @AstroSamantha

Facebook: Samantha Cristoforetti

Karen Nyberg: Space Artist

"No photo does justice to the beauty of Earth." Artist and astronaut Karen Nyberg was reflecting on the magnificence of Earth as seen from a porthole in the International Space Station (ISS). Beneath her, 248 miles (400 km) away on average, Earth was secure under a thin but protective atmosphere. But between Karen and the safety of home was an incredibly inhospitable environment. In space the dangers include:

- Radiation.
- Microparticles and debris traveling upwards of 17,000 miles (27,000 km) per hour.
- Temperatures ranging from minus 250 degrees to plus 250 degrees Fahrenheit (–157°C to 121°C).

Karen knew that space would kill humans instantly if they didn't have high-tech equipment to protect them. Today, as flight engineer for Expedition 36/37, it was part of her job to ensure that her crewmates Luca Parmitano and Chris Cassidy had a safe spacewalk—also known as an extravehicular activity

(EVA). Lucky for them, Karen had been trained well. She understood the many, many safety checks necessary before her two crewmates could enter the airlock. Of course, like anything, things could go wrong. And unfortunately for Luca, something *did* go wrong. It could have cost him his life.

It was July 16, 2013, when Karen helped both crewmates get into their suits. The long process included scheduling time for Luca and Chris to acclimate to the pure oxygen they would be breathing while outside the ISS. Finally, Karen helped them maneuver into the tiny airlock, making sure that the hatch was completely sealed between them and the rest of the station.

Once the two were out of the airlock, Karen didn't have a lot to do to support them. The EVA was scheduled to take six and a half hours, and she wouldn't be needed until they came back in. She took advantage of the time to check some emails, one ear listening to the communications between the two spacewalkers and the flight control team on Earth.

"I feel a lot of water on the back of my head," Luca suddenly reported.

Karen stopped what she was doing and tuned fully into the radio communication. It didn't sound like an emergency—at first. Then, as more water accumulated, the people at Mission Control decided to cut the day's EVA short. As Luca and Chris prepared to come back inside, Luca's communication system faltered. *What's happening?* Karen couldn't know that a large bubble of water had covered Luca's eyes and that some water had also entered his nose, forcing him to breathe through his mouth. If the bubble moved toward his mouth or got any bigger . . .

Things escalated from unusual to dire. Luca and Chris made it into the airlock, but now there were precious minutes for the repressurization process to finish before Karen could let them inside the station and help remove Luca's helmet. She'd already gathered together the Russian cosmonauts, the rest of the crew on the ISS. If something happened, she wanted everyone there to assist.

Karen peered through the small porthole into the airlock. She watched Chris close the outer hatch, a procedure that seemed to be taking too long. By now, Luca's communications equipment wasn't working at all. Karen activated the switch to repressurize the airlock but worried that it would take several minutes. Did Luca have enough time to wait before drowning in the water that had accumulated in his helmet? His body wasn't moving. Was it *already* too late?

Karen's hand hovered over the valve that would accelerate the process. If she sped things up, Luca could take off his helmet quicker. Of course, it would burst both his and Chris's eardrums . . .

Karen stared at Luca, trying to decide. Then Chris reported that Luca had squeezed his hand. *He's okay. He wouldn't be able to do that if he was drowning.* Karen took her hand off the valve and allowed the repressurization to finish normally.

Finally, the process was complete. Karen and her Russian colleagues let Luca and Chris inside. Karen unsealed Luca's helmet as fast as possible. Inside it was bad. At least 50 ounces (1.5 L) of water had collected in his helmet. Luca was okay, but Karen knew that it had been a close call.

The Suit—A Mini Spacecraft

When astronauts go on an extravehicular activity, they wear a complex, body-shaped spacecraft (a spacesuit) to survive the harsh environment of outer space. The sophisticated device is designed for life support and functionality. Each spacesuit—called an Extravehicular Mobility Unit or EMU—is not custom-made for the astronaut but pieced together with differently sized components according to whoever will be wearing it. The hard, upper torso is made from fiberglass. A life support system, worn like a backpack, contains oxygen, a battery, a water-cooling device, a fan, and other critical components. Arm and leg pieces seal onto the torso. To combat the intense cold of space, the gloves contain heaters in each fingertip. The helmet goes on last. A visor, coated with a thin layer of gold, protects against the sun's harmful rays. Because astronauts can spend up to eight hours outside, the helmet includes a pouch of water. By biting on a conveniently placed tube, the person conducting the EVA can remain hydrated.

As a child, Karen was always artistic, learning to sew by the time she was in kindergarten. She grew up in Minnesota in a tiny town called Vining where there were lots of opportunities to make her own clothes. But Karen wasn't just interested in clothes. When she was eight, NASA selected the first female astronauts to become part of the program. As soon as she heard the news, Karen declared to her parents and five siblings, "I'm going to be an astronaut, too." Her family played along. It was a cute announcement, they thought, and there was no harm in dreaming.

Meanwhile, Karen filled her days with everything her small, rural school had to offer. She played in nearly every sport, joined the band, and sang in the choir. At home, she enjoyed making paper dolls and drawing. Often she would sketch pictures of her family or people she saw in magazines. She also kept sewing, getting better and trying more complicated projects.

As she grew up, Karen's pledge to become an astronaut didn't waver. Never mind that she hardly knew anything about space and she'd barely even been away from home. The only big trip her whole family took was one summer when all eight of them piled into the pickup and sat on the wooden benches Karen's father had custom built to fit in the truck's extended cab. The family set off on a road trip to California, into Mexico, and through Texas. It was eye-opening and fun to explore. *Like I'll someday explore space*, Karen told herself.

To the outside observer, it still didn't seem like becoming an astronaut was in Karen's future. She didn't even travel in an airplane until she was a senior in high school and her choir flew to Washington, DC. Then, although she went to college, she wasn't given clear direction about the math classes she needed to become an engineer. Over the summer, she caught up by taking calculus by correspondence (getting and sending all materials through the mail). Finally, Karen got the break she needed.

The University of North Dakota had a cooperative education program. While studying there, Karen earned a spot at Johnson Space Center as a co-op student. She worked for NASA for the following two semesters, and then during the summers while she continued to study. Finishing first her bachelor's degree in mechanical engineering and then moving on to her master's and doctorate degrees, the next logical step was getting a full-time engineering job at NASA.

When Karen had been working for NASA full-time for a year, she applied to the astronaut program. Hoping to improve her chances for selection, she had also picked up a private pilot's license, with 70 hours of credited flying time in a small Cessna airplane. It was a perfect combination of timing, exceptional credentials—and luck—that led to a call from the astronaut office. She was in!

NASA's class of 2000 included 17 astronaut candidates, including Karen's future husband, Marine Corps fighter pilot Doug Hurley. In the new class of astronaut candidates—called

ASCANs—Karen was one of four who didn't have extensive military or pilot experience. She knew she'd have to catch up. That was fine—she was ready to give it her all. Karen began a rigorous schedule of drills and exercises including classes in space shuttle and space station systems and operations. There was also hands-on training.

One aspect of the course was putting the ASCANs in stressful situations to train them to react appropriately. Karen learned to fly a jet, though an instructor was in command of the aircraft. She started in a T-34, a smaller training airplane, and then moved on to the T-38, this one supersonic with a capability of flying over 800 miles (1,300 km) per hour.

Karen also participated in a land survival course. Her group hiked into a rugged section of Maine. With backpacks of essential items, they were otherwise left alone to survive for days in the wild. With no shelter, they had to build their own. Though parts of the experience *were* stressful, to Karen, the training was mostly an adventure and a chance to really bond with the other candidates.

Now a full-fledged astronaut, it would be eight years from the time Karen was accepted into the program to when she would first fly into space. She spent the time in various support roles for space missions and continued with specific training. One particularly demanding challenge was learning to speak Russian, a requirement since Russians cohabitate the ISS. Another intense exercise was spending nearly a week underwater.

NEEMO

The NASA Extreme Environment Mission Operations—NEEMO—takes place underwater. A habitat called Aquarius rests under 62 feet (19 m) of water on the ocean floor, approximately three and a half miles off Key Largo in Florida. The bus-shaped living quarters provide approximately 400 square feet for eating, sleeping, and conducting science experiments. The undersea research station simulates many of the dangers and challenges of living in space. With a team of four crew members and two technicians, participants live for up to three weeks in Aquarius. Aside from prepping for space travel, crewmembers conduct a number of science experiments during their stay. NEEMO is just one of NASA's analog missions—specific training scenarios that strive to replicate the unique conditions of the target environment.

Karen met her teammates at the Miami airport on Monday, July 17, 2006. Over the next two weeks, they would participate in NEEMO 10, spending six days in the underwater habitat, Aquarius. The mission involved conducting various tests in preparation for future expeditions to the moon and to Mars. It was an exciting and vital endeavor, and Karen could barely sleep her first night there.

The next few days were full of safety briefings and preparations for the extended stay underwater. On day three of the training, Karen joined the others as they donned scuba gear and swam down to check out Aquarius for the first time. On the ocean floor, their temporary living quarters came into view and looked like a sunken submarine. Karen also met Lucy and Stella, two resident grouper fish that she would see over and over again during her extended stay underwater.

Finally, the prep work was over. It was a calm, sunny day when Karen dove off the research boat and headed to the ocean bottom. Popping up through a hole in the habitat's "wet porch," Karen toweled off using the chamois towel designated for her. Once inside the cramped quarters, the first task was a safety and procedures tour.

Karen immediately appreciated the many ways that the training would replicate a mission to space. There was the obvious lack of oxygen and the weightlessness outside the habitat, of course, but there was also the experience of working and living in an extremely confined space. Science equipment took up much of Aquarius's main living area. Stacked compact bunks lining each side of a narrow passage comprised the sleeping quarters for the six-member team.

After a quick lunch of dehydrated food mixed with hot water, Karen and a teammate were the first to practice an extravehicular activity (EVA) to simulate conditions on the moon. As Karen dropped into the water, she mused, *I'm officially an aquanaut.* Then she got to work. Today's tasks included testing a new umbilical cord, the line that delivers air from the habitat to each diver. Lighter than previous models that had dragged along the ocean floor, at first it floated too high. NASA engineers solved the problem by attaching strips of lead to the line. Karen was also testing out how to create an appropriate spacesuit for walking on the moon. She wore weights to mimic the moon's gravity and to increase the resistance of walking underwater.

The days settled into a routine, though nothing felt humdrum. There were two EVAs each day, one in the morning and one after lunch. When Karen wasn't involved, she spent time inside experimenting with Scuttle, the remotely operated vehicle—ROV—that would assist on future missions to the moon and to Mars. On day three, she figured out how to manipulate Scuttle to pop into a wheelie to avoid hitting an umbilical cord that was in the way.

Because the environment mimicked the conditions on the moon and on Mars, scientists above the surface had Karen and the team practice maneuvering with various spacesuit configurations. At one point when Karen was practicing falling down, she couldn't get up. "Hey, someone help me up," she called through her radio. It was important to find any potential problems now. On an actual mission to space, there would be no room for mess-ups.

Karen came into the space program at a unique time, just as NASA was beginning to retire its shuttle transports. Not long before they did, she flew in the Space Shuttle *Discovery*. Her mission, STS-124, launched May 31, 2008. During Discovery's liftoff, Karen sat to the rear of the pilot on the flight deck. Behind her in the shuttle bay was the shuttle's heaviest load yet, a hefty 32,000 pounds (14,800 kg). The crew would deliver the Japanese module called Kibo to the ISS.

The Space Shuttle Program: Getting There

The first space shuttle mission was on April 12, 1981, when *Columbia* lifted off from the Kennedy Space Center in Florida. The program completed 135 missions before NASA retired the fleet in 2011. Space shuttles were meant to provide a quick, relatively inexpensive, and safe way to transport astronauts off-planet. In reality, this wasn't the case. The program's worst setbacks were its two trage-dies—when both the *Challenger* and the *Columbia* disintegrated with crewmembers aboard. When NASA finally ended the shuttle program, US astronauts relied on the Russian Soyuz rocket to transport them to and from the International Space Station. Next, with the development of commercial companies, a new method of transportation was suddenly available. On May 30, 2020, astronauts Doug Hurley and Robert Behnken flew in the SpaceX Crew Dragon to the ISS. Commercial spaceflight had begun.

The STS-124 mission was a quick two weeks that passed with lightning speed. With every minute scheduled, there was almost no downtime for anything but sleeping. Optimistically, Karen had brought along some sewing materials in the few personal items she was allowed to bring. Unfortunately, there wasn't enough time to get them out. Instead, Karen's days were packed. One of her jobs was to help manipulate a robotic arm to install the Japanese module. The practice with Scuttle during the NEEMO mission paid off as this required careful and precise movements. Too soon, it was time to go home.

In between Karen's first and second journeys to space, her son, Jack, was born. Suddenly, parenting became a second full-time job. When NASA asked her if she'd be willing to fly to the ISS for a five-month mission, at first Karen had to think about it. Could she leave her son for that long? It was an excellent opportunity, but as a parent, a difficult choice. Ultimately, Karen decided to do it. Jack turned three by the time Karen prepared to launch, this time aboard the Russian Soyuz at the Baikonur Cosmodrome in Kazakhstan.

Though her days on the ISS would be filled with experiments, mandatory exercise, and chores, Karen took along a sketchbook and the sewing supplies she'd brought on the *Discovery*. This time she hoped that there would be an opportunity to sew in space. Luckily there was.

Using scraps of the fabric lining Russian food containers, Karen sewed a dinosaur toy for Jack and a stylized Texas flag for her husband. Next, despite the challenges of sewing in microgravity, she pieced together a quilt square and challenged others on Earth to create star-themed quilt blocks as well. Over 2,400 people contributed squares from around the world. Volunteers sewed these together, and the resulting quilts were later displayed at the International Quilt Festival in Houston, Texas.

When Karen came back to Earth, she brought back several lessons she'd learned. *If Earth is our home,* she mused, *that means that everyone is a neighbor and should be treated as such.* Creating the quilt reminded her of how people all over the globe are connected. Retired from NASA now, as Karen continues to create, to draw and to sew, she views the Earth and its people like a beautiful masterpiece, one that needs our care and respect.

Follow Karen Nyberg Online

Website: https://karennyberg.com/

Instagram: @astrokarenn

Twitter: @AstroKarenN

Anousheh Ansari:
Entrepreneur in Space

Anousheh Ansari was about to embark on the experience of her lifetime. She was in "Star City," the common name for the location in Russia where cosmonauts and astronauts train for missions to space. At the Yuri Gagarin Cosmonaut Training Center (GCTC), there was a ton of preparation for her to go through. And though Anousheh was not part of NASA or any other government space program, she could hardly believe that in a few short days she would be traveling to the International Space Station (ISS).

While keenly interested in supporting innovation and space travel, Anousheh had not trained for years like other astronauts or cosmonauts. Instead, her role in space travel was much shorter term. Anousheh would become the first privately funded female spaceflight participant. She would also be the first Muslim woman to fly to space. A hardworking entrepreneur who was born in Iran but who is now a US citizen, Anousheh aimed to be a role model for both countries during her experience off-planet. First, though, was the dreaded spinning chair exercise.

Privately funded or not, Anousheh needed to go through months of rigorous training to be allowed to participate in this next space mission. Plus, up until a few weeks before her launch, she was a backup for a man from Japan, unlikely to secure a seat on the Russian Soyuz spacecraft for at least a few years. Lucky for her, she got her chance sooner.

Now, Anousheh sat down in the chair that, in many ways, resembled one you'd find in most offices. The difference was that this one had a motor that would rotate its occupant around and around. She reminded herself of the science behind the drill—the spinning chair wasn't meant to be a torture device or punishment for some offense. She assured herself that the quickly turning chair was designed to help her vestibular system—the part of the body responsible for balance and spatial awareness—adjust. Once in the microgravity of space, fluids in the body, especially the ear, were no longer anchored by gravity. She'd learned that feelings of dizziness, disorientation, and even nausea were common ailments for those traveling to space. The spinning chair exercise was meant to minimize this problem.

"Here we go."

Anousheh closed her eyes. She forced herself to solve simple math problems to keep her mind off the unpleasantness of the chair's circular motion. Inside her head, she sang a beloved childhood song, "My Favorite Things" from the movie *The Sound of Music*. She forced herself not to think about the vomit bag the trainers had offered and that she now kept close.

"Move your head left and right," one of the doctors instructed her. Then, "Bend forward and back."

When the drill was finally over for the day—she would do it many, many more times—Anousheh felt relieved. It wasn't until later that a massive headache set in. Her husband, Hamid, asked if maybe she should ask for the next day off. Anousheh shook her head. No. Discomfort didn't matter. What was important was that she was fulfilling a promise she'd made to herself when she was a little girl. No matter what, Anousheh was determined to travel to the stars.

Commercial Space

On October 1, 1958, the US government established the National Aeronautics and Space Administration (NASA). Since then, taxpayers have paid billions of dollars to fund human spaceflight and robotic missions to various locations in space. Until recently, private companies have left off-planet exploration to the government. But that changed when NASA's shuttle program was disbanded in

2011 as a result of catastrophic safety issues. The United States was left with no means of transporting crewmembers and cargo to the International Space Station, except via the Russian rocket, the Soyuz. Meanwhile, several commercial companies began working to design privately owned spacecraft. In 2014, NASA awarded contracts to Space X and Boeing for development of spacecraft to bring Americans into space. May 30, 2020, marked the first successful launch of humans to the ISS aboard a Space X rocket.

Anousheh had always dreamed of traveling to space. Born in 1966 in Mashhad, Iran, she immigrated to the United States when she was 17. Mashhad is an ancient city that was once a center of high learning for math, science, and astronomy. Perhaps this was where Anousheh's love for these subjects first came to her. It was also a time of her childhood that, with plenty of doting relatives, seemed almost idyllic. But things would soon change.

Soon after Anousheh's family moved to Iran's capital city, Tehran, life began to unravel. First, her parents got divorced. While her father remarried, her mother remained single and struggled to give her two daughters the best life she could. For a time, they moved in with Anousheh's grandparents where Anousheh loved to sleep on the balcony when the weather was pleasant. As she peered past the leaves of potted lemon, orange, and jasmine trees, she gazed at the stars and the vastness of the universe. She fell in love with the diamond-studded darkness.

At first, Anousheh attended Jeanne d'Arc school with her sister Atousa. It was an all-girls school run by nuns with instruction in French, Farsi, and Arabic. Then, the rumblings of discontent that had been sweeping through the country began to intensify. The political unrest turned into demonstrations against the government, often violent. Finally, a new regime came into power, and a number of restrictive laws, particularly for women, were put into place. Jeanne d'Arc was forced to shut down.

Anousheh and Atousa were living with their father when war broke out with neighboring Iraq. Food and fuel shortages became a way of life, and Anousheh's father knew it was time to leave. He set his sights on America. The first step was to obtain the proper documentation.

Ultimately, after months of dedication and the heartbreak of initial rejection, Anousheh and Atousa arrived in the United States along with their mother—their father was not initially granted a visa. The three moved in with relatives who lived in Springfield, Virginia, and began their new life. School was especially challenging for Anousheh. It wasn't the academics but the culture and the fact that everything was in English that made it difficult.

"English is your big hurdle right now," her uncle told her. Anousheh promised to work extremely hard—and she did.

That summer she took daily English classes. They paid off. During her senior year of high school, she earned straight A's.

In the United States, Anousheh learned that anyone could go to college, male or female. She applied for loans and took on two jobs, so she could attend George Mason University. Well on her way to earning a bachelor's degree in electrical engineering, she met her future husband Hamid. Two years later, after she graduated, the two were married.

Anousheh told Hamid about her dream to someday visit space. It seemed like an impossible goal as the two, along with Hamid's brother Amir, struggled to earn enough money to buy a house and support their extended family. When the company all three were working for closed its local offices, the Ansaris had no way to pay the bills. After an unsuccessful stint at fixing up and selling used cars, Anousheh suggested they start their own business in the tech industry. The next years were busy and exhausting . . . and while they were making some money, Anousheh was still no closer to fulfilling her dream of visiting space.

Years of intense work finally resulted in success. The Ansaris were able to sell their company, Telecom Technologies, Inc., for a huge profit. Now that Anousheh had a sizable bank account, what would she do next? She thought seriously about applying to NASA, but, already in her mid-thirties, that path to space seemed highly improbable.

One day a man named Peter Diamandis contacted the Ansaris. Anousheh was interested in space, right? Would she like to participate in an endeavor to kickstart the private space industry?

Ansari X Prize

In 1919, Raymond Orteig proposed a contest to advance aviation. He awarded Charles Lindbergh $25,000 in 1927 when Lindbergh became the first aviator to fly nonstop from New York to Paris. In 1996, Peter Diamandis endeavored to model a new competition after the Orteig Prize. His proposal, called the X Prize, would award $10 million to the first team to fly a reusable, crewed spacecraft 100 kilometers (about 60 miles) above the Earth's surface twice in two weeks.

Like the Orteig prize, the purpose of this competition was to encourage innovation. Peter dreamed of jump-starting a space industry funded by private companies rather than by governments. He famously stated, "The day before something is truly a breakthrough, it's a crazy idea." The Ansaris were quickly hooked on the idea. When they donated a large portion of the prize money, Peter renamed the contest the Ansari X Prize. Soon, 26 teams from all over the world entered the competition. The race was on!

When the Ansaris agreed to help fund the X Prize, Anousheh had one condition that was nonnegotiable. She told Peter, "We want the right to purchase two of the first tickets after the spacecraft goes commercial." Suddenly, here was a viable way to reach space. How long would it take private companies to develop their own spacecraft capable of taking passengers? With the incentive of the Ansari X Prize, Anousheh hoped it would be soon.

Anousheh and Hamid traveled to visit the sites of each competitor in the prize. The most promising contestant was a team led by Burt Rutan. His space vehicle, called *SpaceShipOne*, had been financed by Microsoft's Paul Allen. After years of research and testing, Burt's team was finally ready to conduct a demonstration—hopefully winning the $10 million purse. The Ansaris travelled to Mojave, California, where the demo flight would take place.

Launch day was September 29, 2004. Despite the fact that she had barely slept the night before, Anousheh was wired and full of energy. She joined the people who began arriving at the field before the sun rose. Many of them carried their own lawn chairs to watch the demonstration. As more and more people turned up, including actor William Shatner from the TV show *Star Trek*, Anousheh could feel the pulsing excitement of the crowd. Would this day mark the beginning of a new era in spaceflight? Would private space travel soon be available—and affordable—to the general public? Most importantly, was Burt's demonstration today going to work?

Anousheh glanced at Mike Melville, the pilot who would attempt to fly *SpaceShipOne* to the edge of space. Her eyes slid over to his wife and children, and she mouthed a silent prayer that he would return to them safely.

Someone opened the hangar doors where *SpaceShipOne* was prepped and ready to go. The ship was rolled out, now attached to a carrier airplane called *White Knight*. This plane would fly to an altitude of about 50,000 feet and then release *SpaceShipOne*. If all went well, Mike would then engage the rocket engine system in the spacecraft for a vertical ascent past the edge of space—followed by a landing back on Earth. If he succeeded, Anousheh knew she would be one step closer to traveling to space herself.

After one tense moment when *SpaceShipOne* began rolling violently, Mike got the craft under control and pierced the barrier to space. When he eventually glided back to Earth after his historic flight, Mike landed on the centerline of the tarmac. He'd made it! Anousheh's happy tears blurred her vision.

The success of the Ansari X prize helped inspire commercial spaceflight. Several visionaries got to work developing vehicles that could take passengers off-planet. Still, it would be many more years before companies like Virgin Galactic, Boeing, SpaceX, and Blue Origin would be in a position to start selling tickets to the general public for travel to space. In the meantime, Anousheh found a quicker way to fulfill her dream.

The company Space Adventures brokers deals to send private citizens into space. The first Space Adventures client was Dennis Tito, an American businessman who paid approximately $20 million to visit the ISS in 2001. Now it was Anousheh's turn. If successful, she would become the first female and first Muslim commercial space traveler. Anousheh traveled to Star City, Russia, to begin her training for launching on the Soyuz. But she didn't think she'd go to space anytime soon. After all, she was simply the backup for another space participant named Daisuke Enomoto—nicknamed Dice-K—who had first dibs for the next launch. One day everything changed.

"You've probably heard the news." Anousheh listened as the representative from Space Adventures explained that Dice-K had been disqualified due to a medical issue. Anousheh would now take his place—she had three weeks to get ready.

Getting Ready for Space

Regular astronauts (called cosmonauts if from Russia) spend years preparing for a trip to outer space. They must understand the lifesaving systems onboard the space vehicle that transports them to the ISS. Once there, they need to know how to operate and potentially fix each piece of equipment in this space outpost. These space travelers also go through basic medical training—they must take charge if someone gets sick or injured. Then there's the planning they do to conduct a multitude of science experiments—the ISS is a science laboratory in space and hosts a huge volume of critical studies. With so many things that could go wrong, astronauts need a broad spectrum of know-how.

The days flew by. Not only were there more drills, but news outlets picked up the story, and it seemed like everyone wanted to talk to Anousheh. She decided to start a blog. She would continue to write from space, too. "Hello World!" she wrote on September 9, 2006. "A long, long time ago, in a country far, far away . . . there was a young girl who had her eyes fixed on the twinkling stars of the night skies over Tehran."

The day of the launch started at 1:00 AM. Anousheh got up, ate a small breakfast, and, like those who had come before her, she signed the door of her bedroom using a permanent marker. Now there were hours of final preparations. There was also a final goodbye with her family—all of them behind glass so they wouldn't accidentally contaminate her. Catching a virus was not an option. Finally, a bus took her and the other crew—Mikhail Tyurin (Misha) and Michael Lopez-Alegria (L.A.)—to the rocket site. As she lowered herself into her assigned seat inside the cramped module, Anousheh could feel her heart drumming. She was about to experience space!

When the rocket came to life, the trajectory to the ISS was surprisingly smooth. Once above the Earth's gravitational pull, Anousheh loosened her seat straps and looked out the porthole. At her first glimpse of Earth, a tear of joy lifted from her face and drifted through the cabin like a tiny diamond.

Because the process of getting to the ISS took two days prior to 2012, Anousheh slept in the "habitation module" of the Soyuz. Initially she suffered from nausea, a common feeling when confronted with the environmental changes of space. But by the time the crew docked onto the ISS, luckily Anousheh was feeling better. Once onboard, Anousheh and the others were able to video conference with family and friends waiting eagerly—and somewhat anxiously—on Earth. Next, cosmonaut and station commander Pavel Vinogradov offered to take Anousheh on a tour.

The station was still under construction and would greatly increase in size over the next several years, but at the time, it was a collection of linked trailer-like modules that held various science equipment and experiments-in-process. Using handrails to steady her weightless floating, Anousheh scouted out a nook where she would set up her sleeping bag and keep her personal things. Though it was noisy from the constant whirring of a fan, it was the ideal spot because Anousheh could look out a porthole onto Earth.

The eight days passed quickly. Although not part of the professional crew, Anousheh tried to help where she could. She contributed to a few of the science experiments and offered to clean up or do small tasks. She wrote emails, took pictures, and communicated with her family. She also wrote a blog to share with the people on Earth below. It was a precious, magical time, and she wanted to share that feeling with others. Whenever it was time for sleeping, it was hard for her to close her eyes against the stunning backdrop of Earth and space.

Too soon, the experience came to an end. Anousheh managed a tearful goodbye before climbing into a different Soyuz rocket. The journey homeward was much quicker, though rougher, than the launch to space. The reentry and landing made for a rocky, intense ride. The rocket struck the desert in Kazakhstan hard, giving Anousheh a pain in her back. Then, it took days before her body readjusted to the gravity of Earth. It was worth every discomfort.

Anousheh looked back to her cherished time aboard the ISS. She thought of her life on Earth and reflected, "We are here to live life to the fullest and experience it with all our God-given abilities."

Changed, and more appreciative than ever about life on Earth, Anousheh vowed to continue to contribute to the world. Today, she is an entrepreneur who uses various platforms to encourage a better world through innovation.

Follow Anousheh Ansari Online

Website: www.xprize.org

Instagram: @Anousheh_X

Twitter: @AnoushehAnsari

Afterword

It's the final approach. You check with the control tower and then ease the nose of your plane down, monitoring your air speed and any external environmental factors. Now! You've touched down and are speeding down the runway. In moments, you've applied the brakes, decelerated, and taxied the plane next to one of the hangars. On the flight deck, there's no time to relax just yet, however. You still have a series of checklists to go through before you can unstrap and go home. How are you feeling?

Exhilarated? Absolutely.

Exhausted? Maybe a little.

Ready to fly again? 100 percent.

If you're anything like the women in this book, you're fascinated by anything to do with aviation or space. So now what? How do you go from being interested to actually embarking on a high-flying adventure or even a career? Maybe you take lessons like Brooke Roman, eventually working up to flying bush planes in the wilderness of Alaska. Maybe you go the military route like army pilot Tammy Duckworth, air force jet pilot Olga Custodio, or Coast Guard aviator Ronaqua Russell. If space is your goal, you can apply to NASA's astronaut program or even finance yourself like Anousheh Ansari. With the space tourism industry heating up, perhaps a flight into microgravity will soon be much more affordable.

Everyone starts somewhere. A dream is just the spark. Next, it's all about igniting the necessary steps to accomplish a goal. But how? When Tammie Jo Shults watched fighter jets training over her New Mexico home, she told her father that's what she wanted to do. He suggested she talk to a couple of experts. When Karen Nyberg decided she wanted to explore space, she went to college to become an engineer—earning the qualifications necessary to apply to the space program. And Edgora McEwan dropped everything, leaving her family and home, to enroll in a hot-air balloon certification course.

Each one of the women in this book worked hard, sought out opportunities, and asked for help and advice. And no one accomplished anything without faltering at least once. Ellen Ochoa applied to NASA three times before being accepted. Kimberly Scott Russell failed a critical course in college and had to scramble to stay on track. Early on, a teacher told Mae Jemison to switch her "unrealistic" goal of becoming a scientist to becoming a nurse. Finally, petite Katie Higgins Cook had to train twice as hard to accomplish the marine requirement of marching with a 70-pound pack.

It's easy to applaud an accomplishment once it's happened. It's harder to push toward a goal when nothing you've done up to now has pointed you in that direction. The women in this book are inspirational role models, dreamers, and doers who craned their necks upward and chose to fly. They remind us to take hold of our passion, spread our wings, and take flight, too.

Now that you've seen that there is no limit for a determined heart, where will *you* go?

Acknowledgments

What a high-flying adventure and joy this has been! When I first began writing this book, I had no idea of the fascinating, delightful, and life-changing experience it would entail. In my pursuit to find high-flyers, I spoke to incredibly accomplished women. They are women who don't have a moment to spare but spared a moment anyway. Foremost, my gratitude goes to each of you who gave me your time and trusted me to share your stories in this book. Your remarkable accomplishments have inspired me as I hope they inspire young people to pursue their own true passions. A giant thank you goes to smart, dedicated Jerome Pohlen, the excellent editor I have the pleasure of working with for this third time. Thank you to all the wonderful people at Chicago Review Press, including Benjamin Krapohl. Then there's the always enthusiastic, always encouraging James McGowan, my dream agent and hilarious friend. Thank you next to colleagues at Rockville High School. You are all so supportive and fun to work with, despite challenging times (Go away, Covid!). My critique group is another rock, my go-to when the words are wrestling with me and refusing to stay put on the page. Thank you, Laura Gehl, Hena Kahn, and Joan Waites. I learn so much from all of you. Finally, where would I be without my cherished friends and family? Where would anyone be? My love and gratitude to all of you, but especially my beautiful children, my parents, and my husband, who also happens to be my best friend.

Notes

1. Brooke Roman

"But the rewards": All quotes from original author interview with Brooke Roman on November 12, 2020.

2. Tammy Duckworth

"Many people who are": Department of Veterans Affairs, "Assistant Secretary Duckworth Joins US Postal Service for Purple Heart Stamp Ceremony," News Release, May 18, 2009. https://www.va.gov/opa/pressrel/docs/duckworth _purpleheart.pdf.

"I came sideways": All quotes from original author interview with Tammy Duckworth on January 26, 2021, unless otherwise noted here.

"When the only": Tammy Duckworth, *Every Day Is a Gift* (New York: Hachette Book Group, 2021), 101.

"I will always": "Warrior Ethos," Army.mil, accessed January 20, 2021, https://www.army.mil/values/warrior.html.

3. Edgora McEwan

"It was pure love": All quotes from original author interview with Edgora McEwan on November 2, 2020.

4. Dede Murawsky

"It was pure amazement": All quotes from original author interview with Dede Murawsky on November 18, 2020.

5. Anne Macdonald

"I'm getting two": All quotes from original author interview with Anne Macdonald on January 21, 2021, unless otherwise noted here.

Footprints in the snow: Rachel Martinez, "General Macdonald Leaves Footprints in Iraq and Afghanistan," *West Point Women Quarterly Newsletter*, July 2010, https://www .westpointaog.org/netcommunity/document.doc?id=2844.

"Here we are": Martinez, "General Macdonald."

6. Tammy Jo Shults

"Girls don't fly": Tammie Jo Shults, *Nerves of Steel: How I Followed My Dreams, Earned My Wings, and Faced My Greatest Challenge* (Nashville, TN: W Publishing Group, 2019), 27.

"This is career": Shults, *Nerves of Steel*, 27.

Okay then . . . it's not: Shults, 17.

"I felt like": All quotes from original author interview with Tammy Jo Shults on March 17, 2021, unless otherwise noted here.

"a little like": Tammy Jo Shults, correspondence with author, March 31, 2021.

"We're not going down": Shults, *Nerves of Steel*, 230.

7. Katie Higgins Cook

"never climb up": All quotes from original author interview with Katie Higgins Cook on November 9, 2020, unless otherwise noted here.

"There will be no": Ashton Carter, "Department of Defense Press Briefing by Secretary Carter in the Pentagon Briefing Room" (US Department of Defense, December 3, 2015), https://www.defense.gov/Newsroom/Transcripts/Transcript/Article/632578/department-of-defense-press-briefing-by-secretary-carter-in-the-pentagon-briefi/.

8. Olga Custodio

"I waited 10 years": All quotes from original author interview with Olga Custodio on December 9, 2020.

9. Kimberly Scott Ford

"Young men do": All quotes from original author interview with Kimberly Scott Ford on January 18, 2021, unless otherwise noted here.

"Women must try": Amelia Earhart, "Quotes," AmeliaEarhart .com, accessed December 15, 2020, https://ameliaearhart .com/index.php/quotes/.

in 2020 approximately 7 percent: "2020 Active Civil Airmen Statistics," faa.gov, accessed December 21, 2021, https:// www.faa.gov/data_research/aviation_data_statistics /civil_airmen_statistics/.

"It's okay to fail": Kimberly Scott Ford, "A Conversation with Lt. Col. Kim Scott," uploaded by ibrother, Vimeo video, 22:29, accessed December 20, 2021, https://vimeo.com /channels/324060/17130491.

10. Ronaqua Russell

"This is a special": Charles Ray, "Lt. Russell Awarded Air Medal in Tuskegee, Alabama," Defense Visual Information Distribution Service, February 21, 2019, video, 1:38, https://www.dvidshub.net/video/662475 /lt-ronaqua-russell-awarded-air-medal-tuskegee-alabama.

"Due to widespread": "Aviator Delivers Life-Saving Equipment and Personnel During a Hurricane," US Coast Guard Academy, accessed November 8, 2020, https://www.uscga .edu/2019-inductees/.

"I think you": All quotes from original author interview with Ronaqua Russell on March 6, 2021, unless otherwise noted here.

"catastrophic damage": "Saffir-Simpson Hurricane Wind Scale," National Hurricane Center and Central Pacific Hurricane Center, National Oceanic and Atmospheric Administration, accessed October 22, 2020, https://www.nhc.noaa.gov/aboutsshws.php.

11. Mae Jemison

"Houston, Tranquility Base": Erik M. Jones, "The First Lunar Landing," *Apollo 11 Lunar Surface Journal* (May 2018): 102:45:58, https://www.hq.nasa.gov/alsj/a11/a11.landing.html.

"That's one small": Erik M. Jones, "One Small Step," *Apollo 11 Lunar Surface Journal* (April 2018): 109:24:23, https://www.hq.nasa.gov/alsj/a11/a11.step.html.

"Don't you mean": Mae Jemison, *Find Where the Wind Blows: Moments from My Life* (New York: Scholastic, 2001), viii.

"I'm as much": "Mae Jemison, First African American Woman in Space," *Public Broadcasting Service*, broadcast excerpt video, 3:55, originally aired September 22, 2014, https://www.pbs.org/video/makers-women-who-make-america-mae-jemison-first-african-american-woman-space/.

"It's not a question": Ravi Kopparapu, "Life in the Universe: What Are the Odds?" NASA, last modified March 9, 2021, https://exoplanets.nasa.gov/news/1675/life-in-the-universe-what-are-the-odds/.

"We believe that": Miranda Nobles, "First African American Woman in Space Delivers Extraordinary Women Lecture," Auburn University, February 18, 2016. http://www.ocm .auburn.edu/newsroom/news_articles/2016/02/first -african-american-woman-in-space-delivers-extraordinary -women-lecture.php.

"If you think": Jone Johnson Lewis, "17 Inspiring Mae Jemison Quotes," ThoughtCo., last modified January 15, 2020, https:// www.thoughtco.com/mae-jemison-quotes-3530131.

"Never be limited": Johnson Lewis, "17 Inspiring Mae Jemison Quotes."

12. Ellen Ochoa

"T-minus 20 seconds": "STS-56 Launch and Landing (4-8-93)," uploaded by 3210andLiftoff on August 2, 2009, YouTube video, 5:05, https://www.youtube.com/watch?v=RDV-0b0ss_A.

"We have a go": "STS-56 Launch and Landing (4-8-93)."

"I've got a job": All quotes from original author interview with Ellen Ochoa on January 8, 2021, unless otherwise noted here.

"As the first American": Barack Obama, "Remarks by the President at the Presidential Medal of Freedom Ceremony, November 20, 2013," https://obamawhitehouse .archives.gov/the-press-office/2013/11/20/remarks -president-presidential-medal-freedom-ceremony.

"It's one of those": Ellen Ochoa and Howard Wolf, "Deep Space Travel and Beyond with Former NASA Astronaut Ellen Ochoa," May 4, 2019 in Stanford Pathfinders, produced by Stanford Radio, Stanford Pathfinders, 28:00, https://soundcloud.com/user-458541487/deep-space-travel-and-beyond-with-former-nasa-astronaut-ellen-ochoa/sets.

"What everyone in the": Beth Brumbaugh, "Women's History Month Shout Out: Dr. Ellen Ochoa," *Women at NASA*, March 18, 2015, https://blogs.nasa.gov/womenatnasa/2015/03/18/womens-history-month-shout-out-dr-ellen-ochoa/.

13. Samantha Cristoforetti

"It's the saddest": Ed White, "Going Out for a Walk," NASA Education, NASA.gov, accessed February 19, 2021, https://www.nasa.gov/audience/foreducators/k-4/features/F_Going_Out.html.

"I'll be off planet": Samantha Cristoforetti, *Diary of an Apprentice Astronaut* (New York: The Experiment, LLC, 2020), 220.

"We are GO": Cristoforetti, 233.

"When you look": Jonathan D. Woods and Jeffrey Kluger, "Meet the Woman Who Has Spent 200 Days in Space," *Time Magazine*, August 10, 2015, https://time.com/3990462/samantha-cristoforetti-space/.

14. Karen Nyberg

"No photo does": All quotes from original author interview with Karen Nyberg on April 6, 2021, unless otherwise noted here.

"I feel a lot": Tony Reichhardt, "The Spacewalk That Nearly Killed Him: How Luca Parmitano Survived the Scariest Wardrobe Malfunction in NASA History," *Air and Space Magazine*, May 2014, https://www.airspacemag.com /space/spacewalk-almost-killed-him-180950135/?page=3.

15. Anousheh Ansari

"Here we go": Anousheh Ansari and Homer Hickman, *My Dream of Stars: From Daughter of Iran to Space Pioneer* (New York: Palgrave Macmillan, 2010), 108.

"English is your": Ansari and Hickman, *My Dream of Stars*, 34.

"The day before": "Our Team," About Us, X Prize, accessed January 6, 2021, https://www.xprize.org/about/people.

"We want the right": Ansari and Hickman, *My Dream of Stars*, 78.

"You've probably heard": Ansari and Hickman, *My Dream of Stars*, 147.

"Hello World!": Anousheh Ansari, "The Road to Baikonur," *Anousheh's Space Blog*, September 9, 2006, http:// anoushehansari.com/blog/.

"We are here": Ansari and Hickman, *My Dream of Stars*, 230.